PRAISE FOR JUDITH LEPORE

"Judith Lepore has written a powerful account of a harrowing time. It relives the mass destruction wreaked by the McDougall Creek wildfire of 2023, including the devastation of her beloved neighbourhood, Royal Heights Properties. This is a must read, riveting to follow, as the author shares her intimate thoughts; raw, emotional, and very personal. Ms. Lepore bravely allows the reader to enter her mind as she navigates the nightmare she faced..."

J. Harris, Strata President, Royal Heights Properties

"Among the many things I loved about "Finding the Phoenix" is that it gives a human face to these sometimes mainly statistical disasters. You hear about them, read about them, see the numbers of acres burned, and the number of people evacuated, but you just have no concept of what it's like. This memoir made me feel the anguish, the fear, the challenge to one's sense of fairness, one's despair of ever being able to feel secure again. The survivor's guilt, and the way that the ones whose houses were burned down and the ones whose weren't were eventually able to find a way to be together. And the language is so approachable—I felt like I was talking to the author in a coffee shop..."

Beth Johnson, former mayor of Delta, B.C.

FINDING THE PHOENIX

AN EVACUEE'S MEMOIR OF THE MCDOUGALL CREEK WILDFIRE

JUDITH LEPORE

Copyright © 2025 by Judith Hutchinson

All rights reserved.

No part of this book may be reproduced in any form or by any electronic or mechanical means, including information storage and retrieval systems, without written permission from the author, except for the use of brief quotations in a book review.

Cover photo credit:

I would like to gratefully acknowledge Shawn Talbot, a brilliant photojournalist who graciously allowed me to use his stunning photograph for my book cover.

❦ Formatted with Vellum

To my fellow victims of the McDougall Creek wildfire, and the firefighters who fought bravely to keep us safe and save our homes.

CONTENTS

Prologue	1
Chapter 1	3
JUST ANOTHER DAY IN PARADISE	
Chapter 2	8
OUT OF A CLEAR BLUE SKY	
Chapter 3	19
ON THE RUN	
Chapter 4	26
UNWILLING NOMADS	
Chapter 5	35
IN THE KOOTENAYS	
Chapter 6	44
THERE GOES THE NEIGHBOURHOOD	
Chapter 7	51
HOW TO LOSE YOUR APPETITE	
Chapter 8	59
IN THE DARK	
Chapter 9	67
NO REARVIEW MIRROR	
Chapter 10	75
PEACHLAND PONDERINGS	
Chapter 11	81
MORE BAD NEWS	
Chapter 12	85
ONE WEEK IN	
Chapter 13	91
A RAY OF LIGHT	
Chapter 14	96
POISONED JOY	
Chapter 15	100
THE FISHING EXPEDITION	
Chapter 16	105
HOME IS WHERE THE HEART IS?	
Chapter 17	110
BROKEN RAIL RANCH	
Chapter 18	117
THE ENVELOPE, PLEASE…	

Chapter 19 RUNNING OUT OF UNDERWEAR	126
Chapter 20 THE DEVIL YOU KNOW	134
Chapter 21 PARADISE LOST	141
Chapter 22 STANDING IN THE QUEUE	148
Chapter 23 THE MAGIC SCHOOL BUS	153
Chapter 24 AN END TO THE WAIT	160
Chapter 25 TIME TO FACE THE MUSIC	168
Chapter 26 I WANNA GO HOME	180
Chapter 27 SURVIVORS' GUILT	186
Chapter 28 ONE MONTH GONE	195
Chapter 29 HANGING ON	204
Chapter 30 BEING HELD	211
Chapter 31 PICKING UP THE PIECES	217
Chapter 32 FINDING THE PHOENIX	223
Afterword	231
Acknowledgments	233
About the Author	235

PROLOGUE

McDougall Creek wildfire: largest in the history of West Kelowna

Excerpt from *Castanet* **Newspaper, Kelowna, British Columbia**

On Tuesday, August 15, 2023, 6:00 p.m., the McDougall Creek wildfire was identified by the British Columbia Wildfire Service burning at a rapidly accelerating pace ten kilometres north of West Kelowna. At the time of discovery, the fire was listed as less than a hectare (2.47 acres) in size. The cause was unknown and under investigation.

The British Columbia Wildfire Service (BCWS) confronted the fire with an initial team of four ground crew members and accompanying air support, included helicopters and air tankers. Throughout Tuesday evening into Wednesday morning, the team grew to eighteen firefighters, battling to extinguish what was still being described as a small spot fire.

By the time the McDougall Creek wildfire was finally "held" on September 20, 2024, it had grown from less than a hectare to a staggering 13,900 hectares (140 square kilometres), the largest wildfire in the history of West Kelowna.

The BCWS, together with more than 500 firefighters from municipalities across British Columbia and the U.S., were combating the blaze from the ground and air for several weeks.

Overall, more than 35,000 residents in West Kelowna and parts of Kelowna were evacuated, with another 30,000 homeowners placed under evacuation alerts.

Close to 200 properties were completely destroyed or damaged by this devastating wildfire.

I was there.

1

JUST ANOTHER DAY IN PARADISE

On the morning of Wednesday August 16, 2023, I was blissfully unaware of the McDougall Creek wildfire's existence. The beautiful summer day uplifted my spirits, making me even more enthusiastic about my afternoon appointment with a new hairdresser, Bobbi Roper.

Bobbi owns Salon 103 in Lakeview Heights, five minutes away from where I lived. She and I hit it off right away. I loved her lilting Scottish accent and humorous, cosmopolitan attitude toward life. As she deftly applied my highlights, we touched on several topics, including why she had moved to Canada from Edinburgh two decades ago, and why we had moved from the Lower Mainland, B.C., to West Kelowna two years prior.

Another customer came in and took the chair beside mine, and the three of us began chatting. After discovering I had published two epic fantasy novels, the newcomer engaged me in some lively conversation about the bizarre twists and turns of human existence. I decided it was time to introduce myself by name. "I'm Judith."

"And I'm Phoenix," she replied, smiling at my startled expression. "I renamed myself."

"Phoenix," I echoed. "Rising from the ashes…"

She nodded, lifting her eyebrows. "Yep."

RECALLING THAT CONVERSATION WEEKS LATER, I got goose bumps. While we were chatting away in the hair salon, it seemed like just another ordinary day. But, just a few hours later, authorities would put our neighborhood on evacuation alert.

Still ignorant of the impending catastrophe, I went about the rest of my afternoon. There was lots of stuff to catch up on. I had Zoom interviews scheduled with cover designers and editors for the third book in my trilogy, and I was putting the finishing touches on the last few chapters. This is an exciting time for an author, and I was eager to dive in.

Lorenzo, my husband, was also bombarded with tasks (he's a business consultant and realtor) and although both working from home that afternoon, we barely exchanged two words. In fact, it wasn't until almost bedtime that we heard about the wildfire for the first time.

I got the news by text from my next-door neighbour Chantelle:

Hi, are you guys taking this evacuation alert seriously?

What evacuation alert?

Didn't you just get one on your phone?

I vaguely recalled seeing something flash on my phone a few minutes earlier and deleting it, thinking it was more information about the new water treatment plant, or road closures because of construction. Scrolling up to retrieve the message, I wandered out of the bedroom to track down Lorenzo.

He was immersed in his laptop at the kitchen counter, still winding up his dual workday. I sat on the barstool and rapped my knuckles on the counter to get his attention. "Hey! Did you hear about an evacuation alert?"

"No." He looked up in surprise. "Why would we get an evacuation alert? The wildfire isn't here, it's in Keremeos. And it's dying down, thank God. There was way less smoke today, wasn't there?"

It was true. The air quality had been better today than in recent weeks. This had been a bad summer in Kelowna for wildfire smoke, most of it generated from fires burning in surrounding areas like Oliver and Keremeos, approximately 100 km southeast of West Kelowna.

I persisted. "But Chantelle just texted that there's a new wildfire burning near West Kelowna. She says we're on evacuation alert." I stifled a yawn, despite the alarming topic of conversation.

"What else is new? Happy August in the Okanagan!" Lorenzo applauded ironically, adding, "It'll be just like two years ago, no doubt. On alert, then off alert. Better safe than sorry." He peered back at his laptop, frowning in concentration.

He was referring to the White Rock wildfire, which had threatened West Kelowna back in 2021.

We had owned our Okanagan home for two years, keeping our condo in Tsawwassen for the first year and shuttling back and forth for family and business visits to the coast. We sold the condo the following year and moved up full-time in the summer of 2022.

The White Rock fire had been our first close-at-hand experience with wildfire season in B.C.'s interior. For hours, the sky glowed with an ominous orange light, and some residents were briefly evacuated from West Kelowna neighbourhoods; mostly from Glenrosa, about twenty minutes west of us.

An evacuation alert for the White Rock fire was also issued to our neighbourhood. It was kind of unsettling. There had been some damage to properties on the outskirts of Kelowna. But authorities lifted our alert soon afterward, and we were otherwise unaffected.

Nothing came of it—for us. That fact doubtless contributed to how unconcerned we were when the McDougall Creek wildfire evacuation alert came. In retrospect, I don't know why I didn't question it when Lorenzo equated the two evacuation alerts. But at at the time it made perfect sense to me. The power of precedent can create a convincing illusion. And a very foolhardy one.

AN HOUR LATER, Chantelle texted me again.

It's all over the news. Now they say the fire is growing fast and might threaten West Kelowna residential communities by tomorrow. But I never heard of it till now. Tim and Nash are coming home tomorrow, and we really don't want Nash to see a bunch of stuff packed when they walk through the door. Plus I'm tired.

Tim, Chantelle's husband, had taken their seven-year-old son Nash to visit family in Ontario, because Chantelle had undergone painful reconstructive surgery (cancer-related) earlier that week and needed to rest. Another neighbour, Colleen, and I were taking turns bringing her food and helping change her dressings. "The boys," as she called them, were due back the next morning.

Reading her last sentence, I texted back:

Of course you're tired, you need to take it easy. I just talked to Lorenzo, and we don't think anything's going to come of it. But if they don't lift the alert by morning, we'll pack up some stuff. Get some rest and let me know if you need anything.

Ok. TTYL.

Lorenzo had wandered back in with his laptop still open, making me wonder, not for the first time, if he was morphing into a blend of human and AI. "I just looked up the wildfire on *Castanet*," he informed me. "They're saying it's burning out of control. It's doubled in size in less than a day."

It was near midnight. I had given two fitness classes in the morning, taken our Australian Shepherd Oliver for a hike at Kalamoir Regional Park, bought groceries, gone to the hair salon, and made a seafood jambalaya for dinner. I was beginning to slump.

"Well, I'll take my chances and get some sleep," I said, a bit grumpily. "And pack in the morning if I have to. I'm a fast packer."

Lorenzo shrugged in acquiescence and went to brush his teeth. I wandered into the other bathroom and turned on the tap. Looking around, I tried to itemize what to take if we actually did need to leave in a hurry, but soon lost interest.

I glanced in the mirror. My hair looked great. Soft waves, subtle highlights. *Thanks, Bobbi,* I thought. But, out of nowhere, my stomach fluttered.

Residents should be preparing to evacuate...the alert had warned. Even the phrase 'preparing to evacuate' evoked a sense of panic.

Fabulous hair might not be the priority right now.

Re-reading what I just wrote makes me shake my head in disbelief. Readers are probably wondering if I'm really stupid, or just capable of great denial. And I don't blame them. Take this sentence, for instance:

"We don't think anything's going to come of it..."

What a ridiculous thing to say! How would we know? Not being fire scientists, meteorologists, or clairvoyants. But we humans are very adept at denial, especially when it's about things we'd rather not face. What's that you say? Something about *stupidity?* Guilty as charged for being so obtuse.

But a partial defence is that we'd already gone through a wildfire scare that had come to nothing. So, erroneously, we jumped to the conclusion that this scenario would be the same as before.

I have never been more wrong about anything in my life.

2

OUT OF A CLEAR BLUE SKY

Map of Kelowna/West Kelowna

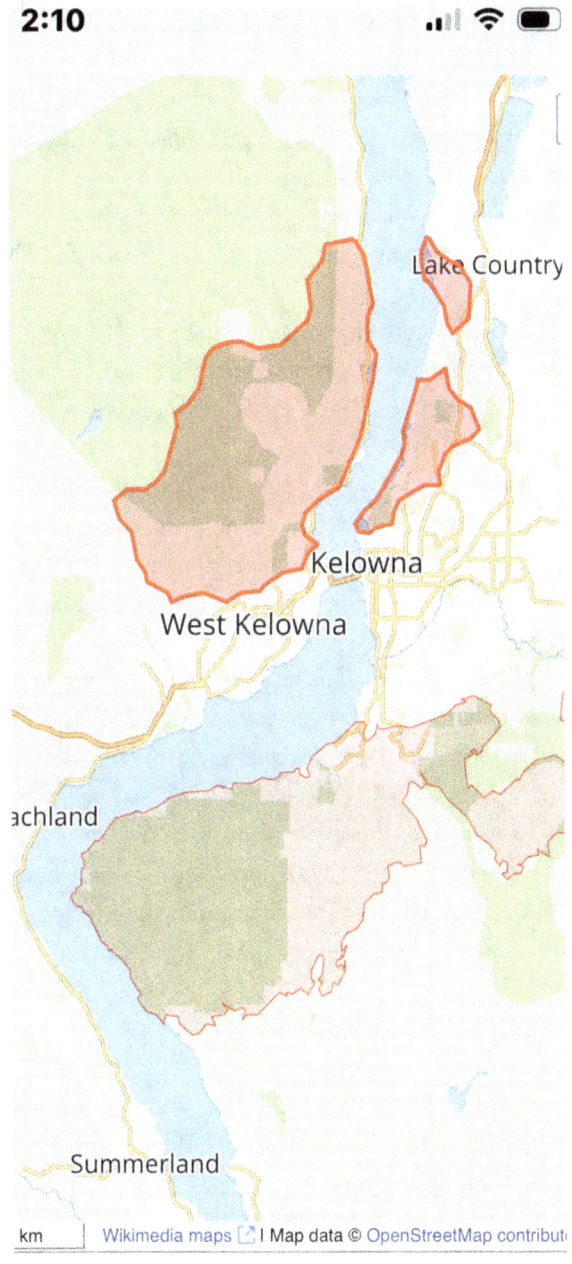

Perimeter of the McDougall Creek wildfire

Excerpt from *Castanet* Newspaper, Friday August 18, 2023

By noon Wednesday, the fire had grown from less than a hectare to four hectares. At 5:00 pm, it had ballooned to 32 hectares and was displaying rank 3 and 4 behaviour.

BCWS incident commander Brad Litke describes to reporters the first few hours of the firefight on Wednesday afternoon and through the night:

"There was an aggressive initial attack on this fire, which was growing alarmingly. The extreme fire behaviour we were observing was due to a dry, cold frontal passage. And with that came a lot of wind—and no precipitation."

BCWS had eyes on the fire, but strong winds and low relative humidity set up conditions for the blaze to spread quickly.

At 8:00 pm, ash and burned debris began falling in West Kelowna. The fire had by then doubled in size again (64 hectares) and was listed by BCWS as a "fire of note."

...Crews had to pull back during the afternoon due to aggressive behaviour. At around 11:00 pm, evacuation alerts were being issued for about 4,800 properties in West Kelowna and on Westbank First Nation land.

Just to emphasize: the evacuation alert we received around 11:00 pm Wednesday night was bewildering—and hard to take seriously—because we were hearing about the McDougall Creek wildfire for the very first time.

WE ARE Judith Hutchinson-Lepore and Lorenzo Lepore, residents of House #7, 1525 Bear Creek Road, in the neighbourhood of Royal Heights Properties, part of West Kelowna Estates, Tsinstikeptum 9, on the lands of Westbank First Nation Tribe (WFN). The WFN is a self-governing band in the Okanagan region of B.C., and is one of eight bands that comprise the Okanagan Nation Alliance of Sylix people.

Royal Heights Properties is a picturesque, horseshoe-shaped cul-de-sac comprising thirty-two properties, facing Okanagan Lake, with a breathtaking view of the lake, the William R. Bennett Bridge, and downtown Kelowna.

The well-built Central Okanagan homes were constructed in the late 1990s. Each exhibited individual style and flair; the yards tended with pride, the gardens landscaped (unless the deer got to them) and welcoming doorway touches.

In other words, Royal Heights Properties (RHP) is a place in which anyone would be proud to live.

Correction: it was.

AFTER A FITFUL SLEEP WEDNESDAY NIGHT, Lorenzo and I awoke at 3:00 a.m., jittery because we had not readied ourselves for possible evacuation. But it was hard to marshal any actual sense of urgency, when no signs of any fire danger had materialized.

As I mentioned, in recent days, Kelowna residents had endured poor air quality and smoke from wildfires burning in surrounding South Okanagan communities. But then, yesterday, a gusty wind had carried all the smoke away, and the sky had turned a brilliant, cerulean blue.

If this new fire was such a threat, surely it would have been broadcast more on the news prior to now, right? Reassuring each other that this had to be a repeat of the wildfire scare last time, we drifted back to sleep.

After more tossing and turning, we got up to face the day at 5:30 a.m. Television and online news reports were ramping up their warning of the fire's imminent danger to residents. Soon afterward, West Kelowna Fire Chief Jason Brolund announced that the evacuation alerts they'd issued for us might very well turn into orders.

And so, although the birds were chirping in the trees and the sky was a stunning shade of blue that mirrored the lake, we began gathering documents, clothes, jewellery, dog bed and food, photos that couldn't be reproduced; along with a few knick-knacks or paintings that were costly or of sentimental value. I contacted my dog-sitter in downtown Kelowna to take Oliver a day early. We'd already booked her for the weekend because we were going away.

The day wore on, and reports from *Castanet* and *Global News* increased in frequency. Everyone was now talking about the McDougall Creek wildfire and how quickly it had grown to 64 hectares (158 acres). With no sign of containment.

No sign of containment?

At around 2:00 p.m., we chatted over the backyard fence with Chantelle and Tim, trying to make a decision. Should we leave now, just in case an actual evacuation order came? That way, we'd avoid a stampede of panicked evacuees. Or should we wait for official word?

Tim looked discombobulated at the prospect of leaving, as well he might, just having arrived home from Ontario. Besides, everything seemed so normal. Looking around, what we saw still completely belied what we were hearing. The sky was cloudless and clear, and the air less smoky than it had been for days. Gazing upward and listening to the finches and robins as they gathered at our backyard birdbath for their afternoon cooldown, I couldn't find a shred of panic in me.

This would come to nothing. Soon, the authorities would rescind the alert, just like last time, and life could go back to normal. We shrugged but still kept sporadically packing... just in case.

In the rest of our little Royal Heights neighbourhood, the jury was also still out. Most people were only half-worried and half-packed.

I remained more annoyed than anxious. The morning had already been wasted, and now it seemed like the entire day was going down the drain. Lorenzo and I had planned to go for a bike ride with friends, a boating picnic with another couple in the afternoon, followed by dinner and a Blues concert in downtown Kelowna that evening. The day was jam-packed with summer fun and adventure, and this sudden evacuation alert seemed little more than an unwelcome and unnecessary annoyance.

The subject of "winds" kept cropping up, though. Meteorologists were saying that sometime mid-to-late afternoon, the air currents would rise and push the fire eastward toward us.

"It looks like it's all going to change in a flash," a newscaster cautioned. The phrase jolted me.

Time to take things more seriously. The belongings we'd selected were lying around in haphazard piles, and now we threw them in boxes which we stuffed into the VW SUV and my little Mazda 3. We turned off the propane and air conditioning, and moved the deck cushions and other obvious fire hazards.

In what I look back on now as a comical degree of denial, we waited until completing all those pre-evacuation tasks before cancelling our plans for the evening. Which we did with reluctance. After all, Papa Dawg was performing at the Blues club tonight. It seemed inconceivable we'd have to miss it.

We decided if we *were* evacuated, we'd take my car and park it at my daughter and son-in-law's place across the bridge in Rutland (East Kelowna), in the visitor's parking lot, and then head toward Kokanee Springs Resort in the Kootenays (by strange coincidence, we'd already planned an out-of-town getaway for the coming weekend). That way, we could pick up the Mazda from on the way home when we returned after the weekend—squeezing in a quick visit with the kids/grandbaby and getting my car back at the same time.

Surely any wildfire hullabaloo would have settled down by then.

I phoned Daria to make sure it was okay. She was on maternity leave from Kelowna General Hospital, where she's an emergency doctor in residence. She sounded harried, and I could hear little five-month-old Maya trying out her lungs in the background.

"I won't keep you," I promised, and filled her in, ending with airy assurances that this would not be a big deal.

"Don't be so sure, Mom," she answered. "People are taking this seriously."

I cracked a joke about *somebody* having to take it seriously, but it wouldn't be me. After blowing kisses to my granddaughter through the phone, I said goodbye and went to water the flowers in the back yard, stopping to chat with our other next-door neighbours, Dan and Mariana Zaretsky. They told us that the relatives who had been visiting them for the past week —including young grandchildren—had left to go to stay with other family in downtown Kelowna.

"Probably for the best," Dan said, quirking his mouth in a smile. "Even if it turns out to be nothing. No need to have a bunch of over-excited kids running around—they're hyper enough as it is."

I was more relaxed after talking to them—Dan had lived in the area for a long time, and seldom got rattled by any wildfire-related news.

Another hour went by with nothing more exciting happening than my beloved stellar blue jay chums landing with a companionable flurry on the fence, waiting for their treats. I lined up a dozen peanuts in a row and had a delightful visit with them before going back into the kitchen.

My favorite, "Stella", stayed on the fence longer than the others, warbling away to me in an insistent way. *Are you trying to tell me something?* I wondered.

Stella had appeared on the back yard fence in the first spring after we took possession of our new Kelowna home. With iridescent blue feathers and a curious gaze, she captured my heart at once.

I've always loved birds, especially so after younger me rescued a white cockatiel from a power line in Vancouver, adopting the fugitive without reservations, and subsequently bestowing upon her the name "Joni Mitchell" because of her soaring soprano riffs.

Stella's vocals were more raucous than Joni's—almost alarming, like she was from Brooklyn or Quebec—but she was very friendly. Within a couple of weeks, she was eating peanuts from my hand and showing up to listen to my fitness class music. Once she even flew into the house looking for me. So, when she disappeared for a couple of weeks, I was upset.

But when Stella came back, the reward was worth the wait. She brought two fledglings with her, awkward and fluffy and adorable. I fell in love with them instantly, naming them Puff and Peepers. They all visited me daily for months, and then Puff and Peepers showed up only occasionally (typical teenagers). But Stella visited almost every day, sitting on the fence and warbling away at me while I gardened or sat in the hot tub.

She was one of my favorite Okanagan buddies.

Bonding with Stella

AFTER STELLA FLEW OFF, I drifted back inside, wondering what else I needed to do. My brain was fuzzy from all the mixed wildfire warning signals. Worry? Don't worry?

I had mostly emptied the fridge, but left the food in the freezer, reasoning that even if the evacuation happened, it wouldn't last more than a day or two. No need to get carried away.

Exhaustion hit me from tossing and turning half the night, and around 3:00 pm I flopped down on the bed for a brief nap. Right before that I checked up on Lorenzo, who'd been trotting back and forth between the yard and garage, deciding what to shut off and keep on (online instructions were contradictory). But most of the urgency had gone out of his actions.

Falling into a brief, deep sleep, I awakened with a start; feeling an inexplicable sense of panic which I tried to dispel by going into the back yard for some fresh air. Blinking, still in a fog, but uneasy.

As predicted, the wind had risen, whipping through the trees and scattering ponderosa pine needles all over the lawn. Our deck chairs had toppled over, along with several flowerpots; petunia petals scattered everywhere. My hair whipped around my face, and I pulled it back, trying to control the wildness.

Looking upward, I got a shock which jolted me out of my post-nap grogginess.

I faced an enormous billowing plume of smoke—its orange-grey cloud funnel hovering menacingly over the ridge of Rose Valley Regional Park, right above our neighbourhood. The gale was pushing it swiftly our way into the innocent-looking blue sky.

This was very different from two years ago. It was like a scene right out of *The Wizard of Oz*.

The McDougall Creek wildfire coming our way…

My heart thudding against my ribs, I turned and ran down the deck stairs to the front of the house. Lorenzo was still puttering in the garage. He saw my face and stopped what he was doing. Waiting for me to speak.

It took me a moment to find my voice. "Time to go," I said. It was 4:17.

The evacuation order for Royal Heights Properties was issued at 5:45 PM, an hour and a half after we left. Our next-door neighbours, Tim and Chantelle, left when we did; Chantelle and I waving somewhat manically at each other from our cars crammed with boxes, kids and dogs. I would later learn that most of our neighbours exited soon after.

I kept looking back over my shoulder as we drove away, zigzagging the hairpin curve which wound down Bear Creek Road. Craning my neck for what might be one last look at my home. My eyes stung and my hands shook.

In the rear-view mirror, I glimpsed Lorenzo's face, faraway

and insubstantial, as he drove the Tiguan SUV behind my Mazda. Beside me on the passenger seat, as if knowing no good was coming from all of this, Oliver panted rapidly, his eyes—one blue and one brown—gazing straight ahead.

We had fled our home.

Watching helplessly from across the lake as the wildfire rampages toward our neighbourhood. (Photo credit Ralph Gardner)

3

ON THE RUN

Surprising ourselves, we were ahead of the surge, getting across the bridge and to downtown Kelowna in just a few minutes. It was a good thing. Within another hour, panicked evacuees would choke the bridge, heading for designated shelter or seeking it in a last minute panic.

Our dog sitter, Lynn, was waiting in front of Okanagan Spirits, the 'gin shop' where she worked in the summers while school was out (she's a teacher at the local college). Lynn greeted Lorenzo and I with a warm smile and Oliver with unabashed delight. "How's my good boy?" she crooned, scratching his ears.

After bonding for a moment, she looked at us. "He's more anxious than usual. How are you guys holding up? This is pretty upsetting, isn't it?"

We nodded, and I tried without success to keep from tearing up. Lorenzo spoke for both of us. "Thanks so much for taking him a day early. We'll be fine. At least we only need to find a place to stay for tonight…"

"You know you can stay with me if it's going to be longer than the weekend…" she began.

"No, no—" I broke in. "It won't be." I halted, wondering why

I had said that with such confidence. *How did I know what was going to happen?*

I hurried on. "We can stay with my daughter, or other friends of ours if we need to. Right now we're just glad not to be inconveniencing anyone."

Her gaze was shrewd. "And you're probably in a state of shock. It's better to have some privacy right now, to process this." Surprised at the insight, I nodded, not trusting myself to speak.

"Well, don't worry about Oliver. Your pooch will be in good hands till you get back." I hugged Lynn and patted my doggie goodbye, and then Lorenzo and I headed back toward our cars. Turning to wave, I saw Oliver watching me, ears pricked up and tail wagging.

As if reading my mind, Lorenzo took my hand in a firm grasp. "Don't worry about Oliver. He'll be fine. Shall we go get a bite to eat before we hit the road?"

We left the cars where they were and walked the few blocks to one of our favourite spots, King's Taps, a lively spot right on the water, with great food and service. A crowd had gathered along the waterfront, everyone looking across Okanagan Lake at the forested hills of West Kelowna—where we lived. There were loud exclamations and agitated gestures. We soon saw the reason.

The funnel of smoke and flame I had seen approaching half an hour ago had enveloped the mountainous terrain of northwest Kelowna. In the deepening dusk, huge pockets of orange glowed on the hillside above our neighbourhood, garish and sinister.

Smoke blanketed the entire area, making it difficult to distinguish houses and other structures. But it was plain to see the woods were burning. And that the fire was terrifyingly close to the houses. My heart caught in my throat.

The West Kelowna hillsides aflame

"Don't look," Lorenzo said. He pulled me away and walked me to the door of the restaurant, propelling me through with a hand on my lower back. "We need to stay calm, grab some dinner, and then get going before bedlam hits."

He waved at a nearby server, and she led us to a table, not attempting to make chit-chat. She must have seen the look on my face.

I struggled to regain my equilibrium, barely registering as Lorenzo ordered beers and burgers almost before we had even settled ourselves in. After the server left with our order, I opened my mouth to speak.

Lorenzo held up a hand. "I know you're not hungry. But we need to eat. And do everything else we can to stay strong. This might not be as bad as it looks. Try not to think about it too much right now."

My husband was demonstrating here his wonderful knack for navigating stressful moments with simple pep talks. He was also right. But it was hard. I ate my burger without tasting it and gulped down the beer like it was medicine, keeping my back to the window.

When we signalled the server for the bill, the manager came over and told us there was no charge for the meal. "You're from West Kelowna, right?" she asked, "And you're being evacuated?"

"That's about right," Lorenzo answered.

"We wish you all the luck in the world," she said. "Everyone's in shock about how big this wildfire is and how fast it's moved. This must be so hard for you."

I gaped at her, twisting my napkin with my fingers. It was unsettling that complete strangers were feeling so sorry for us. It made me feel like something *really bad* was happening, and I didn't want to accept the fact.

But this woman was regarding me with such sympathy brimming from her warm brown eyes, and she'd given us a free meal, with no hesitation.

I wasn't ready to be a victim, but there was no need to be rude. "Thanks," I mumbled.

"Come on, honey," said Lorenzo, "Let's go."

Baby Maya was sleeping when we arrived at Daria and Sean's townhouse. I'd pulled my little car into the driveway so I could store the few precious keepsakes in their garage. But the skittish look on Daria's face told me now was not the time for a detailed curation of our wordly goods.

"Here's the car fob," I whispered. "You can go through the stuff and decide what to keep in the car and what to put inside." She gave me a thumbs up and a hug. "Where's Sean?" I asked, keeping my voice low.

"He's doing some errands and then heading to your place." I looked at her in confusion. "Sean wants to turn your sprinklers on—in case it helps. We just heard on the news they might be barricading Westside Road soon."

"What?"

Westside Road was a major throughway that turned off the highway, then passed our exit (Bear Creek Road, our street) before continuing north to Bear Creek Park, Trader's Cove, Fintry and La Casa. It was a long, frequently used, stretch of road.

"Why barricade it?" I could hear the stammer in my voice and tried to steady it.

Daria's eyes welled up. "Mom," she said gently, "This fire is dangerous, and it's spreading really fast." She paused. "You already know this, it just hasn't sunk in. Just stay safe, Mom."

"You, too." I turned to go, then whipped my head around. "You don't think the wildfire's going to spread to Kelowna, do you? You guys are safe here, right?"

She waved her hand. "There's a lake between us and the fire, Mom. Don't worry. But West Kelowna's a different story. I got a text from a fellow medical resident who lives on the West side, with a one-month-old. They're on alert but haven't been evacuated. I'm on her list of places if they need somewhere to go."

"Good." *My God*, I thought. Imagine evacuating with a newborn. "Text me every hour..." I blurted. She rolled her eyes, and then gave me a long, contradictory hug.

I waved a second goodbye and walked toward Lorenzo, who was waiting in our SUV, engine idling. His eyes were worried. *Let's go...*

As I got in the car, my mind whirled with images, bombarding me in rapid succession: The view from across the lake of the hills above our home aflame. Sean driving toward our house right now (was he safe?) Oliver's head cocked to the side as he watched me walk away. And babies being wrapped in blankets as their parents fled their homes—it all assailed me, piling up until I thought I would have an anxiety attack.

Driving down Harvey Avenue to get to Highway 33 ,we saw the orange and grey roiling cloud once more, and the bridge— thronged with vehicles of evacuees departing West Kelowna. The fear in the air was almost palpable.

"Here's our exit." Lorenzo turned off the main road, and then we were heading down the highway toward the Kootenays; steeling ourselves for a three-hour night time drive to an unfamiliar motel in Christina Lake. Knowing it would be hard to sit still for that long, because we were both ready to jump out of our skins.

~

At 7:00 pm, we listened on the car radio to a hastily convened news conference in which West Kelowna Fire Chief Jason Brolund warned the public that the McDougall Creek wildfire was expanding exponentially, blazing toward residential areas and becoming a very real threat to homes. The wildfire was living up to the hype.

A terrified urgency gripped me. It was as if the wildfire was a malevolent entity that would pursue us wherever we went.

~

We heard later that our son-in-law Sean hadn't been been able to access our property and turn on the sprinklers. The police had already blockaded Westside Road by the time he got there.

Hours afterward, R.C.M.P. detachments, law enforcement officers from Westbank First Nation, and West Kelowna firefighters attended the affected neighbourhoods to ensure everyone had evacuated their homes. When they reached Royal Heights Properties, however, they'd found a glitch. The power to the automatic gate had been shut off and it was closed, blocking the entrance. Worse still, some residents were still there and there was no other way out, putting them in a potentially terrifying situation.

By fortunate happenstance, our other next-door neighbour, Dan had still not left, although Mariana had. Another lucky thing was that Dan was part of the strata council, in charge of maintenance. He was able to manually open the gate—otherwise firefighters and police would have had difficulty getting in to our development, which was the last thing they needed.

Dan told us later that by the time he left, the air was thick with smoke, and embers were flying all around him. As he drove through the gate, it suddenly became very dark, although night had not fallen.

In other words, things were happening quickly in our neighbourhood as we sped down Highway 33. But we were oblivious to how much more was in store.

BY THE TIME we got to Christina Lake, the McDougall Creek wildfire had jumped the Rose Valley neighbourhood and snaked up Westside Road, creating a swathe of panic and destruction. And it was blazing its way up toward West Kelowna Estates. Where we lived.

What we had dreaded was taking shape as our new reality.

The wildfire begins to menace residential neighbourhoods
(Photo credit: Alex Kassimatis/Castanet Newspaper)

4

UNWILLING NOMADS

Lorenzo and I had decided to move to Kelowna later in life, after all our kids had grown, but before we'd fully retired. We were in our sixties, and hoped to drift smoothly into part-time work and full-time fun in B.C.'s beautiful Interior, away from the Lower Mainland's increasingly chaotic environment.

The Okanagan was an obvious choice. We had always been drawn to its rustic, untamed vibe. As an adolescent, I had lived in Vernon and Kamloops for a couple of years and carried with me vivid memories of gleaming lakes and majestic, untamed wilderness. In his younger years, Lorenzo had also travelled in the Kelowna area for business and team sports, and had fallen in love with it for the same reasons.

Besides the fact that it's stunningly beautiful, the Okanagan is also a practical place to live, being very affordable compared to Vancouver. Our dream became a concrete plan.

Lorenzo has an ongoing project management contract in Vancouver that allows him to work remotely, for the most part. My freelance writing and fitness training careers in Tsawwassen had spanned thirty years, but going forward I was hoping to pursue my longtime dream of writing and publishing fiction.

All our kids and grandkids (my daughter, son-in-law, and granddaughter, and Lorenzo's son and three daughters and five grandchildren) lived in B.C. within a few hours of us, even with our move to the Kelowna area.

In 2017, we commenced our search in Penticton, gradually inching our way through Summerland and Peachland, seeking the perfect home that "ticked all the boxes." Three years after beginning the search for our dream home, it appeared in West Kelowna, almost out of the blue, in February 2020.

It was a lovely open-concept house with a spectacular lake view—one of the most important 'boxes' to be ticked. Situated in West Kelowna Estates at the top of a hairpin curve on Bear Creek Road, it beckoned to us the moment we saw it.

One of our neighbourhood's chief charms is that it is the best of both worlds, giving an illusion of being perched above it all, with breathtaking lake and city views, surrounded by dizzyingly steep hillsides and flower-carpeted gorges. When, in fact, Royal Heights is only a five-minute drive to downtown Kelowna, and eight minutes from the hospital.

The distance to the hospital I learned the hard way soon after we moved here, when I sliced my thumb open peeling potatoes while staring entranced at a stellar jay outside my kitchen window.

Our new home's roomy front deck overlooked the lake. Someone who must have been an expert gardener had beautifully landscaped the back yard. In spring and summer, it transformed into a lush paradise of flowering plum trees, lilacs, climbing hydrangeas and mountain ash trees, rosebushes, and wild raspberry canes; a paradise inhabited by a flotilla of sociable stellar jays, nervous quails, and elusive hummingbirds.

The kitchen island faced the lake, so I could chop veggies while feasting my eyes on the shimmering blue water. There was also a spacious ground level suite, an appealing mortgage helper. In other words, the house had everything we could hope for, so we didn't hesitate. After making an offer that same day, we became the new owners of House #7, 1525 Bear Creek Road.

Proud new homeowners

A couple of weeks later, the COVID-19 pandemic struck, and the world changed.

When we finally moved to West Kelowna full-time, we realized how lucky we were to have sealed the deal before the pandemic changed the rules. Other friends and family who entered the housing market during those years needed to tackle the myriad challenges of restricted travel regulations, masks and distancing, and fear of contracting COVID while selling or buying a new home. At least one couple we knew purchased a house sight unseen except for a virtual Zoom tour.

Our excitement at becoming permanent residents in Royal Heights was unbounded. We couldn't get enough of the lake view and wildlife wonderland: deer walking down the street, curious chipmunks, bold jays, and once in a while a bear (our street 'Bear Creek Road' wasn't so-named for no reason).

An extensive network of trails wound down the surrounding hillsides, magnificent for hiking in the summer and snowshoeing in the winter.

Lorenzo snowshoeing on our trails—steps from our front door.

In spring the hillside bloomed with colour—arrow leaf balsam (otherwise known as Okanagan sunflowers) sporting vivid yellow petals, scarlet poppies carpeting the ground beneath the massive ponderosa pine forest; alongside delicate purple lupin and white yarrow dotting the in-between areas, with their delicate pastel shades. I always returned home from a hike with a bouquet of wild flowers.

In our own front yard there were massive hydrangeas with creamy white blossoms, and fragrant lavender, which attracted bees and other useful pollinators. I tried my hand at growing sunflowers and it was crazy, the flowers grew to the size of my head…or bigger.

Growing sunflowers bigger than my head

Then there was the fireweed, which I'd seen nearby areas like Rose Valley Regional Park, where there had been a fire in recent years. None around our place, though.

When we were deciding whether to purchase, we'd asked the current owner about wildfires, and they assured us there'd been no fires in our neighbourhood in all the years they'd lived there. Staring up at the massive pines looming over our backyard, I wondered why. But the lack of fireweed, and our neighbours' lack of concern, gave me confidence there was nothing to worry about.

Looking back, these factors shouldn't have created such a sense of false security. Just because something hasn't yet happened, doesn't mean it won't, right?

FINDING THE PHOENIX

∽

As we drove down Highway 33 in the deepening twilight, the sky glowed an eerie shade of amber. I kept glancing back, but other than the oddly-tinted sky, I could no longer glimpse any trace of the tragedy that was unfolding behind us.

We were in the Kootenays, nearing Christina Lake. The Kelowna radio stations were all static now, so I scrolled down my phone, looking for online news on *Castanet's* website. Castanet Newspaper was Kelowna's primary online news source, and had excellent reporting.

My heart contracted as I read the latest reports.

Excerpt from *Castanet* Newspaper, Aug. 17, 2023, 9:30 pm

All West Kelowna Estates and Rose Valley residents must leave immediately! That's the latest evacuation order from Central Okanagan Emergency Management (CORD) as the McDougall Creek Wildfire continues to spread into the night.

Evacuees should register online or head to Royal LePage Place at 2760 Cameron Road. The Vernon Emergency Operations Centre has also been opened at Kal Tire, 3445 43rd Avenue in Vernon, to accommodate permanent residents of West Kelowna who have been forced from their homes this evening.

"Vernon!" I exclaimed. "Why are they opening up an emergency centre that far away?"

Lorenzo glanced at me and shrugged; his eyes reddened with fatigue. "Maybe they're just preparing for any eventuality." My stomach roiled. How bad was this wildfire getting? And how much worse was it going to get? I thought of who we'd left back there: Daria, Sean, Maya, and Oliver.

Bleak and silent, we pulled into the parking lot of the Christina Lake Motel, where we'd booked the only remaining room in town. After unloading our essentials for the night, we switched on the television and were just in time to catch the 10:00 edition on *Global News* B.C.

We sat on the edge of the mattress and stared at the screen, aghast. The cameras were showing live footage: a seething wall of flame as it engulfed *our neighbourhood*. We were right at the epicentre of the fire.

McDougall Creek wildfire from across the lake (Photo credit: Gregory Dahms/Castanet Newspaper)

"I can't believe this is happening," I choked. "Our house is somewhere in there—probably burning down right now..." Tears clogged my throat and I couldn't say any more.

"It's all just *stuff*," said Lorenzo, his voice steady. "We can replace stuff. I'm with the person I want to be with. That's all that matters." He put his arm around me and pulled me close.

That worked, for about two minutes.

Later, *'It's all just stuff'* would become one of our mantras, although repeating the phrase didn't always do the trick. That night, however, images of the rampaging wildfire consumed my emotional perspective, leaving little room for anything else.

Our cell phones were ringing non-stop—Lorenzo's kids phoning from the coast, along with my mother and brother in the U.S. and other friends and relatives. They'd all been watching the shocking events unfold. Seen the same footage we had. We couldn't help concluding, with only the merest shadow of a doubt, that we had lost our home.

Daria called, speaking in a near-whisper so as not to wake

Maya. Her voice kept breaking as she tried to find words of comfort. At the same time Sean was texting, saying the same thing Lorenzo had. That it was just stuff—we still had each other... The words cracked through my numbness, and I started sobbing.

Hours later, Lorenzo and I curled together on the motel bed, exhausted, listening to the clanking whir of the ancient air conditioning unit within, and a pack of coyotes outside our motel, their ominous howls sounding apropos: like demented prophets yodelling an ominous warning of the approaching apocalypse.

It was no lullaby, but we gave in to our exhaustion and fell into a fitful sleep.

Excerpt from *Castanet* Newspaper, Friday August 18, 2:38 am

The McDougall Creek wildfire remains very active and unpredictable. Significant structural loss has been confirmed.

It was disorienting enough to wake up in an unfamiliar motel room in a strange town. Although I should add that Christina Lake is quaint and lovely, and I'd go back there in a heartbeat—if I wasn't worried about getting flashbacks of that terrible first night of our evacuation.

But upon awakening, we were instantly bombarded with news updates about the horrific growth of the McDougall Creek wildfire. This was so overwhelming that I wanted to pull the quilted coverlet over my head. The statistics were appalling.

Already the worst on record, B.C.'s wildfire season had spiralled into a crisis state. In a single day, this new fire had forced the evacuation of over 10,000 West Kelowna residents (within a few days more, the number would grow to a staggering 35,000 evacuation orders, with another 30,000 evacuation alerts pending). It was raging through residential streets and burning homes with terrifying speed and ferocity, giving the occupants little time to escape.

Worst of all, B.C Wildfire Services seemed nowhere close to being able to contain the destructive inferno that just kept growing and growing, like a monster out of a Stephen King movie.

Shortly afterward, West Kelowna's mayor Gordon Milsom declared a state of emergency.

Mayor Gord Milsom declares a state of emergency for West Kelowna

Federal and Provincial orders providing support to the affected communities quickly followed. A centralized Emergency Operations Centre (EOC) led wildfire management and community support in the Central Okanagan.

The coyotes were right. An apocalypse was descending. Would the province just keep burning till there was nothing left but wasteland?

Fast forward: two weeks later, on September 3, 2023, the McDougall Creek Wildfire had morphed from 300 hectares to 13,712 hectares (33,883 acres). 35,000 residents would have been evacuated from their homes, with 30,000 more remaining on evacuation alert.

Thankfully, we had no idea that was going to happen as we huddled in our little room at Christina Lake Motel.

Things were bad enough already.

5

IN THE KOOTENAYS

Excerpt from *Castanet* newspaper, Friday, August 18th

At a hastily called news conference Friday August 18th, West Kelowna Fire Chief Jason Brolund declared that Thursday night had been "one of the most challenging nights of firefighting in our history," going on to say it was like "100 years of firefighting all at once." Visibly shaken, he added, "This is a fire chief's worst nightmare."

Friday morning, we gulped down a quick breakfast of fruit and coffee before leaving Christina Lake. We had little appetite. The TV was on, and we couldn't tear our eyes away from the images of destruction that were flooding in. Worse yet, our neighbourhood was so blanketed in smoke it was impossible to tell if our house was still standing.

West Kelowna home goes up in flames (photo credit Ralph Gardner)

Lorenzo and I wedged ourselves into the overcrowded VW Tiguan and prepared to burrow deeper into the Kootenays, where at least we were safe for the time being. But even though we were increasing the distance between ourselves and the wildfire, our unease grew. The threat of losing our home was something we couldn't outrun.

A framed Robert Bateman painting of a wolf (Lorenzo's favourite) poked into my shoulder from the back seat. I shoved it away, bitter, thinking *I'm too old for a Woodstock type adventure*.

But we had no choice, since this 'adventure' was forced on us. And although safe from the fire itself, we couldn't escape its enormous footprint. Within the next hour, heavy smoke descended on the entire Central Okanagan. And even here in the Kootenays, it surrounded us like a suffocating shroud.

It's hard to describe if you haven't experienced it, but in a wildfire-affected area the atmosphere is different, the light dimmed even in midday, and in the air an unpleasant chemical tang which lingers in the back of your throat.

This toxic pall persisted even after we had put a few hundred kilometres between us and the fire, only dissipating when we arrived at Kootenay Bay. But the smoke mantle turned out to be a double-edged sword: it masked the fire's activity and the destruction it caused, but also brought somewhat cooler temperatures and light winds.

Driving the last few kilometres, we had listened to the news with a mixture of hope and trepidation. Evacuation orders continued—they would do so all day Friday, and into the weekend. Upwards of 20,000 people were now forced from their homes, double the number from the last update. Meanwhile, the West Kelowna fire department frantically strove to contain the raging beast of a wildfire.

"Turn it up, please," Lorenzo said. "What are they saying about 'spotting'?" He was rounding a sharp corner just past Greenwood, so I reached over and cranked up the radio volume.

That's when we learned about another frightening development: the McDougall Creek wildfire had spotted or 'jumped' the lake to downtown Kelowna, which was on the same side of the lake as my daughter and family, and also Oliver and his dog sitter Lynn. Too close for comfort. With shaky hands, I texted both Daria and Lynn and confirmed everyone's safety.

I had never heard the terms "spotting" or "jumping" to describe fire behaviour before, but I would soon know much more than I could ever wish to. The quick definition is that embers from a rampant wildfire can fly a very long way, sometimes even across an enormous lake. True story.

Incredibly, there were soon reports of a third spotted fire burning in Lake Country (a community to the north of Kelowna) and friends of ours also phoned from Wilden (northeast Kelowna) to say there were spot fires in their neighbourhood and they'd received evacuation alerts.

Heading east through the hellish smoke, we reached the outskirts of Nelson and drove toward the ferry terminal in Kootenay Bay. From there we would catch the ferry to the eastern shore of Kootenay Lake, where the small community of Crawford Bay nestles in the Purcell mountain range. There lay our next destination: the golf resort I'd booked all those months ago, anticipating a carefree weekend.

The radio was still blaring at full volume, and we heard some astonishing news. Kelowna International Airport had just been closed. B.C. Wildfire Service air support needed the airspace.

They'd closed the airport. That announcement confirmed it for me. We were in some kind of world-ending crisis. Lorenzo was more pragmatic in his thinking. "It's the smart thing to do," he said. "The water-bombers and reconaissance aircraft take priority. And who wants to be coming here right now, anyway?"

Water-bombers combatting the wildfire (Photo credit: Ralph Gardner)

It was mid-afternoon, and really hot out, but the smoke dome shrouded the atmosphere so much that we could barely see the sun—it was like a persistent solar eclipse. I kept blinking, imagining we had landed on some otherwordly place, like Mars or Jupiter.

I checked *Castanet* Newspaper on my phone again, and read more updates, each more horrifying than the last. I reached my limit after reading that newspaper photographer Nick Johansen had just witnessed half a dozen to ten homes consumed by flames in the Westside Road area.

It was like someone had punched me in the stomach.

"We don't know for certain that ours is one of them," Lorenzo said for the tenth time that morning, his mouth setting in a stubborn line. He is an eternal optimist, and I sometimes roll my eyes at it. This time I wanted more than anything in the world to believe him, but it seemed less and less likely that our home had survived.

PULLING INTO THE FERRY TERMINAL, I was stunned to see that there was no trace of the smoke pall that had pervaded everywhere else. It seemed impossible, miraculous.

The sky was a brilliant blue, and the sun beamed down in buttery golden splendor. A frolicsome breeze gusted along the little harbour as we stepped from the car. Was the wind keeping the smoke at bay? I decided the reason didn't matter, and just inhaled the fresh air in deep, grateful breaths.

Colourful boutiques and coffee shops lined the ferry dock. Even better, there was a self-described 'legendary' ice cream stand, where we ordered an espresso flake waffle cone so huge that we couldn't finish it, even though we were sharing.

Lorenzo bought me a flowy summer dress at a boutique (called *Blue Sky* of all things) while we waited to board the tiny ferry. At any other time, I would have been enchanted. As it was, I welcomed the distraction from anxiety.

An enthusiastic young guy sporting a Molson Canadian baseball cap announced that boarding had begun, and we returned to the car. After informing us this was the longest free ferry ride in Canada, he waved us onto the boat. He seemed so proud we couldn't help grinning and giving him two thumbs-up. On that cheerful note, we made the Balfour/Kootenay Bay ferry trek over to Crawford Bay, and Kokanee Springs Golf resort.

Six months earlier, when I'd booked this weekend at Kokanee Springs Resort as a belated surprise birthday gift to Lorenzo, I could never have dreamt what would transpire: that on this weekend we would be fleeing a wildfire. That we might lose our home. It was surreal.

The clear skies and fresh air continued throughout the brief trip. I gazed at Kootenay Lake, entranced by the choppy waves and churning foam as we chugged along.

Being on the water with a fresh breeze on my face was pure bliss. It was a reprieve, however brief, from the veil of smoke, from air which was so dry it seemed to scorch the lungs. And from the bleak vision emblazoned on my brain, of orange flames consuming wooded hillsides. My delight was a little disproportionate, making me realize how desperate I'd been for sanctuary.

Looking back, I have often marvelled at the timing of our readymade shelter in the Kootenays, far from the panic and fray. We were far more fortunate than many of the evacuees, who had to jostle for space to stay in a panicked and suddenly overcrowded city.

WHEN WE DISEMBARKED, our brief, ice-cream fuelled euphoria disappeared like a fragile bubble popping. The light quality had reverted to that unnerving monochromatic grey haze, something conjured from a dystopian sci-fi novel.

Checking in was going to be awkward. I opened the discussion with my usual diplomacy. "There's no frigging way I'm golfing."

Lorenzo's eyebrows shot up so high they almost hit the roof of the Tiguan. "You think *I* want to golf?"

"You always want to golf." I knew I sounded sullen.

"Not being a robot," he retorted in a scathing tone, "I couldn't take part in a golf tournament while knowing our house might be burning down. Or already gone."

"Oh." I paused. "Sorry." He closed his eyes like he was in pain, and I put a tentative hand on his knee. "I don't know what I was thinking—maybe you might want the distraction?"

"Well, I don't."

"Duly noted," I said. He squeezed my hand, and we both stared straight ahead for a few moments. Without any preface, an exquisitely graceful doe pranced out of the woods and across the road, far enough ahead that Lorenzo didn't have to brake. I gazed at her, glum; missing home so much it was like a physical ache. Seeing deer on our street (and in our yards) was a daily occurrence on Bear Creek Road.

Dispelling these thoughts with difficulty, I returned to the problem at hand. "It's going to be weird, though. Checking in. Explaining why we're here but not joining in the tournament. Maybe they'll give us the cold shoulder."

"Stop worrying about it!" Lorenzo struck the steering wheel, sounding exasperated. "People listen to the news here, too. And besides, checking into the resort isn't going to be the weirdest thing that's happened in the last twenty-four hours."

"True." I dropped the subject. Lorenzo's jagged tone signalled me that even though he'd been doing a good job of holding it together, his stress level had almost reached the breaking point. It reminded me we needed to be kind to ourselves and each other. We were embroiled in a catastrophic situation, and had clicked into 'crisis response' mode. But we had very different ways of coping.

At least we'd agreed on 'no golf,' so the first thing we did as we plunked our bags down in the resort lobby was to withdraw from the couples' golf tournament. I am an abysmal golfer, so my absence would be no loss to anyone. I felt bad for Lorenzo, though. He would have enjoyed it.

The front desk clerk's eyes widened when I said we were from West Kelowna and were evacuees of the McDougall Creek wildfire. At the look of pity on her face, I almost burst into tears. Instead, I shrugged. "Our hearts just aren't in this right now."

"Of course they aren't!" she exclaimed. "This is just terrible what's happening! Everyone is gobsmacked. Consider your golf cancelled, and you'll get a full refund. Is there anything else we can do?"

(Shout out to the staff at Kokanee Springs Resort. Their sympathetic response and unswerving courtesy that weekend bowled us over).

It turned out there was another good reason besides emotional turmoil to cancel golf. The air quality in the Kootenays had gone from bad to worse. Smoke was blowing in from every direction as the province of B.C. almost literally 'caught on fire.' The weather network had just warned people to stay inside, because the air was saturated with toxic particulates from multiple wildfires.

But you'd never know it. That was another new thing I learned during our evacuation, interesting and sinister. When the air quality in a wildfire vicinity is at its worst, there often isn't even a whiff of smoke in the air.

I'd always thought that being near a wildfire, you'd see and smell smoke like you do when toasting S'mores over a campfire, but, nope! Apparently, the most harmful particles are so small they're undetectable, by sight or smell.

Even so, it was dangerous to breathe even for a short time, let alone four hours on a golf course. We started clearing our throats and coughing within moments of walking back outside. But of course that didn't stop some of the avid golfers. Which explains why we found ourselves amid a bunch of resort guests merrily whizzing around in golf carts or returning from the green, talking about their game. It was hard to believe. Weren't they getting the same air quality alerts that we were?

But we had other things to worry about, like getting settled in our room. Entering, we barely registered how nice it was—picturesque and cheerful, with a rustic view of the woods and a cozy sitting area. Birds were twittering away right outside our window, but we ignored their serenade. In what was already becoming a routine that would last throughout our evacuation, we turned on the TV to the local news station as soon as we'd dropped our bags on the floor.

It was more of the same. The fire was an indomitable wall of flame, consuming vast tracts of forest and threatening neighbourhoods, sometimes obliterating them.

Reports came that the winds had pushed the fire upwards, south and west, where the insatiable blaze had blasted like a fire-breathing dragon through West Kelowna Estates, including Bear Creek Road.

Our street.

I covered my face with my hands. This confirmed it. Might as well face the truth. We were going to lose our home.

6

THERE GOES THE NEIGHBOURHOOD

Excerpt from *Castanet* **Newspaper**, Saturday August 19, 2023
   Firefighters across the province have poured into West Kelowna in the past few hours to help battle the fire. "We are an army out there," said Fire Chief Jason Brolund, referring to 127 structural firefighters and 91 fire trucks working in the community.

Our cell phones were blowing up.

Pacing the length of our cozy room at Kokanee Springs Resort was beginning to get claustrophobic, so we opened the sliding glass doors out to the small deck and circled each other, taking turns; inside, outside. I preferred outside. The moonlight was nice. Something to howl at.

We were fielding a multitude of concerned calls and texts from apparently everyone we knew on the entire planet. It saved my sanity to ignore some, prioritizing Royal Heights neighbours, and close family and friends. I began reading a text from Chantelle, who was trying to hide her panic from seven-year-old son, Nash. The emojis weren't pretty.

At least Nya and Olivia are with their mom, so it's more stable for them right now. Especially since it's in downtown Kelowna, away from the fray. But Nash misses them.

She was referring to Tim's two teenaged daughters from a previous marriage who lived with them part time.

How are you feeling? I texted back. *How's the soreness?*

I was worried about her terrible body bruising from the reconstructive surgery; unable to erase the image of her limping out of their house, carrying a duffel bag with Nash's stuffed giraffe's head sticking out of it.

I'm not worried about the soreness in my body. It's the sore heart that's hurting...

I had a strong urge to go to her, give her a hug. Tell her how unfair this was. We could both cry. Then laugh and make a cup of tea. Talk about how strong we were and plan our next hike with the dogs along the hillside trails. Which were probably burning right now, even as we texted.

Now was not the time for tea.

Hang in there. I paused, not knowing what else to add. Even though I'm a writer, words had fled my mind. Words had evacuated my brain.

Lorenzo's phone buzzed. "Dan," he informed me, before picking it up. Dan Zaretsky is the next-door neighbour who'd been able to open the main gate manually when the electronics failed, enabling firefighters and police services to enter our development.

Shooting the breeze with next door neighbour Dan on our deck before the wildfire

IN NORMAL TIMES calm and measured, I could hear Dan's voice escalating like the whistle of a train hurtling down a dark tunnel. His sentences ran together almost incoherently as he and Lorenzo talked about what the doorbell cameras were showing. Listening to this disturbed me; it was so out of character.

The whole doorbell camera thing had been a sore point. Right before evacuating, we'd shut off our power, based on instructions Lorenzo had found online. So now we couldn't access our camera footage, which was frustrating.

Lorenzo paced up and down the room, shaking his head as he listened. "Oh, no!" he exclaimed, stopping stock still with the phone to his ear. His eyes were wide as they met mine.

"What?" I yelled, unable to control myself, stamping my foot with impatience.

"Just a sec," Lorenzo said into the phone, and then looked at me, a muscle in his cheek twitching. "Steve and Tracy's house is on fire. Dan can see it on his camera."

I stared at him, stupefied. The house he was talking about was right across the street from ours, with a nearer view of the lake, perched above the lower cul-de-sac.

Steve and Tracy hail from Australia. For the previous six

months, they had been renovating their home to accommodate their aging parents, who had just sold their own home in Australia. Right before the wildfire erupted, Steve and Tracy had returned from abroad with her parents in tow, all ready to move into their new Canadian abode.

Now it was ablaze.

My heart was beating so hard it was booming in my ears, and Lorenzo's next words sounded tinny and faraway.

It turns out that West Kelowna firefighters were there at that very moment, trying to extinguish the blaze. The fire had blasted up Westside Road from Trader's Cove, flames licking their way through the forested hillside and consuming huge long-standing tracts of forest—where I walked Oliver every morning along the trails. Our house was at the top of the street (along with Dan's and Marianna's, Steve and Tracy's, Chantelle and Tim's). We were the closest to the woods that were now burning out of control.

Unbeknownst to us—because no-one's doorbell camera was facing it—the home at the very top left side had caught fire already and was burning to the ground, along with its adjoining garage and two cars within.

The owners, Aleda and her husband Joseph, didn't know either. They were away when the evacuation order came. That was also the case for several other neighbours in Royal Heights Properties. After all, it was the height of summer, and many people were away.

Fast forward to several weeks later. After returning to our neighbourhood, I walked past Aleda and Joseph's property and witnessed one of the strangest sights I have ever seen: the burned-out metal shells of their cars, looking like rust-coloured skeletons, one complete with a recognizable car radio jutting out from the interior.

Aleda and Joseph's house was kitty-corner from Steve and Tracy's. We were all a stone's throw from each other. It was probably a good thing we didn't find out right then. Hearing about even one burning house in our neighbourhood had upended our world.

I took deep, gulping breaths, reminding myself that at least firefighters were on our street, battling the blaze.

Lorenzo and Dan were still conversing when my phone buzzed. It was our neighbour, Raj.

Raj is a lovely twenty-eight-year-old with an M.A. in Epidemiology, who lived with her mother, Sutha, and worked for Interior Health. Sutha was a teacher nearing retirement. Their house was right next door to Steve and Tracy's.

I gulped.

After a few seconds of staring at the phone, I walked out onto the small balcony to avoid the chaos of competing with Lorenzo's phone conversation. My palms were sweaty as I hit the button. "Hi Raj," I said.

"Judith?" Her voice sounded small and fragile.

"Where are you?" I tried to recall our last conversation amid the jumble of goodbyes between neighbours.

"With my friend, in downtown Kelowna," she reminded me. "I wish Ramu was with me, but he's better off in Florida with my mom."

I remembered now. Sutha was in Florida visiting her aging grandparents, and had taken their small dog, Ramu, with her. Her dad was in India on a business trip.

"That's true," I agreed. "It's stressful for the pets." I had a stab of longing to bury my hands in Oliver's fur and gaze into his devoted eyes.

"Yes." She didn't sound relieved, though. There was a long pause.

"Have you talked to your mom and dad?" I asked.

"Yes. They're very worried about the wildfire reaching our neighbourhood."

"Of course." There was another fraught silence. My heart wrenched. This poor girl was dealing with this frightening evacuation ordeal by herself. "Are you okay, Raj?"

"No, Judith." Her voice had become even smaller. "I am watching on my doorbell camera." She choked on a sob. "Steve and Tracy's house is on fire."

I cleared my throat, which had suddenly tightened. "Yes, I know. Lorenzo is talking to Dan. He says he's also watching—the firefighters are working hard to put it out."

"Well, tell him to look again. The firefighters are running down the street now. They cannot control the fire." Raj began crying. "Judith, I think I am going crazy. I think I am having a breakdown."

"Don't look anymore," I blurted; operating on instinct. "Put your phone down, Raj. Watching it is what's making you crazy, because there's nothing you can do. Put your phone down and go for a walk."

"It's hard to do, Judith." Her voice quavered. "I don't know if I can stop watching."

"You have to," I urged. Fear for her wellbeing gripped me. "Is your friend there?" I asked. "Can I talk to her?"

There was no reply. "Raj?" I repeated. For a moment longer there was silence, and then I heard her sharp cry.

"The tree in front of our house is on fire! It just caught a piece of flaming wood from Steve and Tracy's house." She was crying again. "Our house is going to burn, Judith."

"Turn the camera app off, Raj." I dug my nails into my hand to keep from crying along with her. "Can you do that?"

"Okay," she said, surprising me. Her voice became calmer. "I turned it off. I will not watch any more. It's not good for me."

"That's a smart decision." I walked back inside, almost colliding with Lorenzo, who had ended his call with Dan and was wandering around aimlessly. His concerned look when he saw my face made me realize how distressing these last few minutes had been. I waved my hand in an instinctive effort to block out our eye contact. I couldn't handle it right now. If I kept looking at him, I might drop to the floor in the foetal position and just stay there.

"Call me whenever you need to, Raj," I said into the phone, sounding as normal as I could. "You're talking to your parents all the time too, right?"

"Yes," she replied, hesitantly. "But my mother is so upset. I don't want to worry her too much."

The answer to that would have been way too emotional. I settled with, "Take care of yourself."

After this dismal end to our conversation, I put my face in my hands and remained that way for a while. Wondering how this would end for us. Not really wanting to know.

7

HOW TO LOSE YOUR APPETITE

Although drained and sick at heart, primal needs took over as Lorenzo and I realized we were famished. Our shared ice cream cone seemed in the distant past by now. We took ourselves to the resort restaurant.

In a fragile frame of mind, I was a bit blindsided when we entered the place. To put things in perspective, this was the peak of a B.C. summer in the Kootenays, where nothing bad had happened to anyone else. The atmosphere was energetic and upbeat. People were chatting about the golf tournament, the iconic resort, the beauty of the surroundings.

All of which was great. For them. They weren't going through what we were going through. Of course, most people would have heard about the McDougall Creek wildfire in West Kelowna. But no one could understand the enormity of our situation, and this realization made everything seem far worse. Looking around at all the happy campers, I felt nauseated and wobbly on my feet.

Being in a crisis and surrounded by those who aren't is like being on a desert island. Talking to our neighbours, listening to the news in West Kelowna, gave us a deep connection to our community. Not just as a geographic location; but also at this moment a community of need, coming together with shared emotions. We could help each other get through this. It was a faint glimmer of hope. Of "Finding the Phoenix."

I recalled again the woman at the hair salon on Wednesday—three days ago—a hundred years ago. Phoenix. "Rising from the ashes?" I'd asked, with a facetious smile. Now it seemed to be my pre-ordained mantra for hope. Finding a way through the darkness.

But there was no way we could do it alone.

THE SERVER who led us to our table was a buoyant young man with a long ponytail and a charming Aussie accent. "Hiya, folks! I'm Devin. Hope your day's been a blast. What can I get ya to wet your whistles?"

We mumbled an order for IPAs and settled our eyes on our menus. I picked the first thing I saw, Margherita pizza. Lorenzo decided on a bison burger, and we stared into space while waiting for Devin's return. This was out of character for us, both of whom have worked in the "people" business for many years. Normally we'd be making friendly small talk with everyone who crossed our path. But right now socializing was the furthest thing from our minds.

It seemed urgent that we eat and leave as soon as humanly possible. Otherwise, unable to 'fake it', I might have a humiliating break down in public. My fingernails dug into my palms, and I worried I might lose it at any moment.

Just then Lorenzo's phone buzzed, and he picked it up. "It's Pierre," he mouthed.

Pierre and Colleen Schaaf own House #3, three doors down the hill from us to the south. We had become good friends—they were the ones we were supposed to go to the Blues concert with when we received the evacuation order.

These neighbours live in West Kelowna in the spring and

summer months, and in Edmonton the rest of the year, because that's where their business is, and their kid and grandbabies. When the evacuation order came, they naturally headed back to Alberta to wait things out, so Pierre was calling us from Edmonton. Sweat broke out on my forehead. Did they know something we didn't?

"Hey," Lorenzo muttered into the phone, "we're in a restaurant grabbing dinner. Can I call you back?" He paused, then said "Okay," and hung up.

"What's going on?" I asked.

"I don't know. He's been watching the footage on his doorbell camera like everyone else who can. He's going to text me."

Devin came back at that moment and put our beers down with a grin and a flourish. We hastily ordered, trying and almost certainly failing to match his friendliness. "I shall return!" he declared with a bow. But Lorenzo was already looking at his phone again, reading Pierre's texts.

"He's a few minutes behind on the footage. It's showing Steve and Tracy's place on fire."

"Of course." I couldn't refrain from sarcasm. "That's old news..."

Lorenzo continued to read the text. "But now it's looking completely torched—and huge chunks of burning material are flying everywhere!The firefighters can't salvage it. Pierre says they're heading down the street. Wait..." He paused, his eyes widening. "Pierre says they've stopped in front of Sutha and Raj's place. The tree in the front yard caught a flying ember, and it's on fire. It's candling!"

"I know all this..." I began, before remembering Pierre was watching his doorbell camera footage a few minutes later.

Lorenzo waved his hand for me to be quiet. "But the footage shows the firefighters stopping—trying to put the tree fire out... Hey, they did it! Now it shows they're leaving again..." His voice shook, and I knew that, like me, he must be picturing it in his mind.

(Weeks later, we learned that the firefighters' astute and courageous act of stopping to put out the flaming tree in Raj's front yard saved their home).

Lorenzo began texting back. I clutched my mug and took a gulp of beer, which tasted very good, suddenly. "What are you guys talking about now?"

"I'm asking Pierre if anyone can see *our* house with their doorbell camera," he replied tersely.

Unfortunately, because of our house's location, only Steve and Tracy could see our property. And their house was burning down. So I knew Lorenzo's fact-finding mission was pointless. But there was no point in starting that conversation.

"Oh well..." I said, raising my mug again, thinking I should have gone for tequila instead of beer. "Do we *want* to see our house in real time? I mean, look what it's doing to Raj. The sheer stress of it."

"Of course I want to see. It's the devil you know!" Lorenzo's brows knitted as his cell buzzed again. "Oh..." he breathed, his voice trailing off as he read a text. He put his hand over his eyes.

"Is it our house? *Is it?*" My voice had risen with each syllable, sounding at the end like a pathetic squeak in my ears. "Tell me!"

He answered in a hoarse voice. "It's next door—Chantelle and Tim's place." He waved his phone in front of me, so erratically that I didn't have a chance of seeing it. "Sutha's doorbell camera caught this—Nash's wooden playhouse in the back yard, it's caught fire, gone up in flames."

"Show me," I whispered.

Hollow-eyed, he handed me his phone with the screenshot Pierre had sent.

Nash's playhouse burning

NASH WAS seven years old when the evacuation order forced him from his home. Slender, tow-headed, and blue-eyed, he is an adventurous little boy.

Before the fire, he was always whizzing around the neighbourhood on his bike or scooter, with a friend or two following close behind. Leading the pack. Or jumping on the trampoline, playing baseball in the backyard with his parents, accompanied by the enthusiastic yapping of their little Yorkie, Jax. One of his favourite summer activities was hanging out in his wooden playhouse.

Which was, at this moment, burning to the ground.

I had forgotten about our home for the moment. "Where are the firefighters? Maybe one or two haven't left yet. They just put out the tree fire at Raj's place... could they put this one out, too? I mean, how hard could it be? It's not a full size house, it's a child's playhouse!"

Even while saying these words, I realized they made no sense, and I must have sounded hysterical. My shoulders had started shaking, and I put my hands on them to stop.

Lorenzo was already texting. The phone rang, and he held up

his hand. "It's easier to talk than text. I'm just going to take it outside for a minute." I nodded.

He strode outside and I could see him pacing around the grounds, kicking at the grass tufts with his summer loafers. Outdoors looked grey and dull, not reflecting any of the turmoil and suspense we were going through; and I wondered if this was how religious people envisioned purgatory.

I bit the inside of my cheek and tapped my fingertips on the table, trying not to replay in my mind what I had witnessed and couldn't erase: a little seven-year-old's playhouse being reduced to ash.

"Here's your grub!" Devin had appeared like a benevolent Aussie genie, but his cheerful announcement fell flat, and seeing this, he whomped the plates down and hustled away, muttering "Enjoy..."

Enjoy. That word had become alien to me. It boggled my mind to reflect that only a couple of days ago, we had all kinds of fun things planned for the next few hours, days, weeks. But it had all gone up in smoke (literally)... and forty-eight hours later, here we were, not knowing whether we even had a home to return to.

Lorenzo came back in and sat down. He looked at me, then picked up his fork and poked at a yam fry, scraping aside the aioli in distaste (he hates mayonnaise). A moment went by.

"What else?" I prompted. "Do Tim and Chantelle know about the playhouse?"

"Yes, they know. They're trying to keep it from Nash. Tim told the girls, and they feel so sorry for him. Chantelle says they were all bawling together on Facetime after Nash went to bed."

Thinking of Tim's perky daughters Nya and Olivia grieving for their little brother's loss, my eyes welled up. I told myself they would have had to find out sometime. And, unlike Nash, they were old enough to understand it, at least a bit. But even us adults were having a tough time processing this.

I chewed my lip, afraid to ask the question. "Their actual house isn't on fire, though?"

"Not yet. But the odds are good."

"I *know* the odds are good." I glared, so angry I could have thrown my pizza at him. "But if it hasn't happened yet... I just want to hang onto some hope, for God's sake!"

Devin walked by us, glancing sidelong at our intense faces, avoiding eye contact.

"Did Tim say anything else?" I asked in a whisper, staring at my pizza, not in the least bit hungry anymore.

"No. Just that the smoke is getting thicker, which means the fire likes our neighbourhood—it's not going away anytime soon." Taking a desultory bite of his burger, Lorenzo chewed, doggedly and without pleasure, as if taking the last bite of many in a hot-dog eating contest. He gestured to my plate. "You need to eat something."

I nodded, picking up my pizza and dipping it into his discarded aioli, munching with the same lack of enthusiasm as he had. Washing it down with beer helped, though, and I finished a second slice before his phone buzzed again. He looked down. "It's Dan."

"What's he saying?"

Lorenzo paused.

"All the doorbell cameras have gone black. The power's out."

"So then no one knows what's going on anymore." I stared at him, but he didn't reply. There was nothing to say. The McDougall Creek fire had claimed our neighbourhood.

I began to cry silently, tears coursing down my cheeks. Lorenzo patted my knee under the table, squeezed my hand; and then shook his head at me, frantic. He hates scenes of any kind. But I couldn't stop.

Devin walked by us, pacing with slow steps. Then again, the other way. Finally, Lorenzo raised his hand, beckoning him over to the table.

"Is everything okay, mate?" Our server tugged his ponytail, nervously.

"I just wanted you to know," Lorenzo told him, "My wife and I are not arguing. We are not getting a divorce or anything of that nature."

"Ah…" Devin looked polite but confused.

"It's nothing like that—it's just that our house is probably burning down right now."

Thinking back on this now, remembering Lorenzo saying the words without a trace of humour or irony; and seeing the mixture of bafflement and dismay that appeared on poor Devin's face, I laugh. I really do.

But, from that night on, it was a long time before I could laugh again about anything.

8

IN THE DARK

We tipped Devin generously to compensate him for the awkward experience of serving us. He looked dejected when he cleared our plates, murmuring something about how he kind of understood, there being lots of wildfires in Australia, too, and it's so devastating, isn't it? Which made us feel a bit guilty. But we were more exhausted than anything, and when we returned to our room, we collapsed into bed and fell asleep on top of the covers.

The next morning we sat on the velvety couch in our hotel room and watched the news, dull-eyed and disbelieving.

Part of trauma's torturous cycle is continually alternating between realization and denial. Grasping reality amid a calamity can be very difficult, mostly because you don't *want* to grasp it.

In this case, watching news reporters talking in horrified, pitying voices about the 'flood of evacuees' made me shake my head in sympathy—until I remembered, for the fiftieth, or the one hundredth time—that we were them.

Which reminded me: we were checking out of the Kokanee Springs Resort today. The fact that neither one of us had addressed our next stay speaks to the trauma-based denial I was just talking to you about.

As if snapping out of a trance, I turned to Lorenzo. "Well, fellow evacuee, where are we going to go now?"

We began discussing the option of staying at a hotel, using insurance company vouchers. We were reluctant to do it, for several reasons, the main one being the fact that we had a dog, and not a small one. Oliver needed space or he got anxious.

With serendipitous timing, my phone buzzed. It was Paula McLaughlin, my longtime friend from Tsawwassen (our kids had graduated together, and then the McLaughlin's daughter Angela and Daria had gone on to attend U.B.C.). She and her husband, Peter, had relocated to Peachland several years ago. After Lorenzo and I moved to Kelowna we got back in touch, getting together for lunches and dinners, or going to concerts and plays with each other or with our husbands.

We often marvelled together about how lucky we were to be living in the beautiful Okanagan. Right now, not so much...

How are you doing, Jude? Were you guys evacuated from the wildfire? This is just awful. I can't believe it's happening. The smoke is so thick here in Peachland we can barely see a thing, and we're twenty minutes away from you! What's it like in West Kelowna...or dare I ask?

Yes, we're evacuated 😢 *. We're not anywhere near Kelowna, though. We're in the Kootenays. Ironically, I planned this weekend months ago as a birthday gift to Lorenzo. So, we're out of the fray for now...*

But if you're still evacuated after the weekend, where are you going to stay? With Daria?

No, they've offered to shelter another medical resident and their one-month-old newborn. We were hoping to be back home by then, but now it looks like we might not have a home to go back to.

OMG. There are no words for that. Just prayers. And please, please, please, come and stay at our place. You'll have it all to yourselves! We're going down to Vancouver tomorrow

night. It's perfect timing. We'll be gone for a week, and hopefully by then this will all be over.

I started to respond, then thought of something else.

Can we bring Oliver? Our dog sitter could only take him for the weekend.

Of course.

Relief flooded me. "We're going to Peachland tomorrow," I informed Lorenzo, noting his drawn face and glazed eyes. He gave me the thumbs up; not asking any questions, which was unusual for him. It was as if he had put himself temporarily on 'pause.'

I smiled, a bitter, inward smile. If only we could hit *'rewind'*...

THE NEXT MORNING dawned with no sun anywhere in sight, except for that eerie orange ring caused by the high dome of smoke. According to the weather experts, the air was too saturated with toxic particles to be outside, so we couldn't even go for a stress-reducing walk. Trapped in the room, we texted with our neighbours.

Chantelle responded to me before 7:00 am:

OMG. **What a terrible night. We've stayed the last two nights with friends of ours downtown, and the bedroom has no door, so we had a real lack of privacy thing going on. Also, we were trying to act normal around Nash so he wouldn't worry, and so we had to whisper and gesture every time we wanted to talk about what was going on.**

I was having a moment where I refused to accept this wildfire thing was actually happening to us. But the image of Chantelle's place on the doorbell video footage wouldn't go away. I texted back with unsteady fingers.

That must be so nerve-wracking.

The last recording on the doorbell cameras was Nash's playhouse burning down.

Tears pricked my eyes. *I know.*

I could almost feel her dread through the phone. Even before this evacuation, Chantelle had been navigating several challenges. Her recent (painful) reconstructive surgery followed a mastectomy the year before, after being diagnosed with a rare form of breast cancer. On top of that, she and Tim were juggling the chaotic existence of a blended family—besides their young son Nash, Tim's two teenaged daughters lived with them part time. Not to mention the dog and cat…

As if that wasn't enough, Chantelle had been threatened and intimidated at her workplace (she's a mental health worker at Interior Health) after inadvertently incurring the wrath of a deeply troubled client. Convinced she was persecuting him, he'd threatened and then began stalking her. A restraining order was now in place, and she'd been put on stress leave as well as medical leave. Not fun.

Now this wildfire.

Try to stay calm. What a lame thing to say, I thought.

She texted back. 😤**Where are you guys going next? You're only there till tomorrow, right?**

Yup. Thankfully, our friends in Peachland offered their place—and it's empty!

Lucky you. I bet the bedrooms even have doors.

Hang in there! ❤️

Talk soon… 👍

I stared at our text thread; grateful we'd left Oliver with Lynn for the last couple of fraught days. He was a sensitive dog and would pick up instantly on our anxiety. Trying to hide such intense emotions from your kids—or your pets—was almost impossible. Thinking about Chantelle and Tim's situation, I sent a silent prayer of gratitude to the universe that my daughter's home was in Rutland and had escaped the fire, even after it jumped the lake.

My eyes stung, so I put down my phone, rubbing them. Too much texting? Or were the smoke particles permeating everywhere? Seeping through every tiny nook and cranny, trying to suffocate us. Once again, an irrational fear gripped me that the wildfire was a malevolent demon, chasing us with personal intent wherever we went.

"Pierre says he and Colleen feel guilty for not being there to band together with everyone," Lorenzo told me, quirking his mouth as he stared out the window. He swung a mock golf drive off an imaginary tee; something he did a lot, but it looked incongruous now, adding to my sense of unreality.

"That's ridiculous," I replied. "They shouldn't feel guilty. Edmonton is their home base. It made total sense for them to go back there instead of scrambling to find shelter here. And just like with us, they left more space for evacuees who have nowhere to go."

"I told him that. But he still feels guilty. Logic isn't the ruling emotion right now. As you know."

"What's that supposed to mean?" I muttered, poking him in the ribs. But even though I was affronted, I knew he had a point. Restlessness and claustrophobia kept hitting me in waves. Every few minutes, I felt like I was going to have a panic attack. Lorenzo was also jittery, his imaginary golf swings more frequent and erratic. After another hour of pacing and texting, we were desperate enough to opt for a walk outside, regardless of the dire air quality warnings.

UNBELIEVABLY, despite the air quality danger advisory, the golf tournament was still going full steam ahead. Determined golfers bustled around, only some of them wearing masks, but all of them glancing uneasily up at the bleak metallic sky.

Ignoring them, we struck up a narrow path winding through a wooded hillside. A creek burbled alongside the trail; its water level so low the water barely covered the rocks. It had been a dry summer.

The sound of rustling wings came from above, in the branches of a giant ponderosa pine tree. I peered up to see a raven regarding me with a skeptical gaze. Its wings looked odd. Instead of the usual glossy black, they were grey and sooty. And so was its head—looking like ash had rained down upon it.

As I stepped closer, incredulous, it cawed defiantly and took off. But even the belligerent caw seemed to carry a note of fatigue and desperation. I wanted to call after the ashy raven, to say *I know how you feel—I'm so sorry you're going through this...* But by now it was only a black dot in the distance, continuing its tremulous journey into the unknown.

We walked for about fifteen minutes, then, in a moment of disheartened unison, turned and headed back toward the resort. On the way, we stopped in at the pro shop, wandering in a surreal haze among the shirts and skirts and skorts, tagged with enticing sales discounts that signalled the end of summer.

"Hi, I'm Gina!" a salesclerk said in a friendly voice, waving a ballpoint pen at me. Aqua-framed reading glasses perched on her nose, and she had been peering through them while briskly marking the end of season sales prices on the golf wear. I gave her a despondent wave.

"Looking for anything in particular?"

"Nope," Lorenzo said, "just killing time."

"Ah..." She paused. "You two are the wildfire evacuees from West Kelowna. How's it going? This fire just keeps getting bigger and bigger, doesn't it?"

It was a rhetorical question—all anyone was talking about was how the fire was growing out of control.

"Terrible," I replied. No point in sugar-coating it. "We're in the hardest hit area, and we've been evacuated from our home for who-knows-how-long. If it hasn't burned down, that is. And it probably has. This wildfire is like an unbeatable monster—it just keeps getting bigger."

Listening to my own words made the situation seem more

real than I wanted. I shuddered and felt Lorenzo's arm coming around my shoulder.

Gina grimaced, shaking her head. "I know. I heard it's up to 10,000 hectares now. That's almost 25,000 acres! 100 square kilometres! Even with all the firefighters and water bombers and everything they're throwing at it..." She stopped abruptly, looking at my face, which I knew had crumpled, then asked tentatively, "So, there's no word on *your* house yet?"

Lorenzo squeezed my shoulder. I couldn't look at him, but I pictured him closing his eyes the way he did when he was getting a migraine. "No," he answered for me. "The doorbell cameras went out last night. But before the fire cut off the power, we could see that the house across the street was burning down, and the fire was blazing pretty good in our next-door neighbours' back yard, too. I'd say the odds are good our house is gone."

Hearing my optimistic husband say these words in such a desolate voice struck me like nothing else since seeing the fire swoop down on West Kelowna last Thursday night. My vision blurred with tears, making Gina's shirt look like a blob of peach sherbet. I couldn't believe we were talking to a total stranger in a golf pro shop about our community being destroyed.

There was a long silence before Gina responded. "When are you leaving?" She rammed her reading glasses up her nose in an almost angry gesture.

"Tomorrow morning."

"We'll have the restaurant make you up sandwiches for the road," Gina said briskly. "And there will be no charge for your stay here. In fact—" she held up her forefinger as if struck by a sudden epiphany, "if you need to stay longer, that's fine too—stay as long as you want. No charge."

Turned out, Gina wasn't a salesclerk, she was the Owner Relations Manager of the resort. Her swift and sympathetic response was astonishing. But we would soon find out that this kind of thing was happening all over the place—people coming together to help those in crisis.

And there is no question about it: receiving compassion and support in a catastrophic situation puts you on the road to recovery—wherever you happen to be. In the case of the McDougall Creek wildfire, I call it my first concrete step in Finding the Phoenix.

9

NO REARVIEW MIRROR

Excerpt from *Castanet* **Newspaper**, Sunday August 20, 2023

Canada Task Force 1 arrived in West Kelowna today and began counting damaged properties. There are close to 500 firefighters now battling the fire, and crews are finally starting to make progress.

"We have access to resources on an unprecedented scale now. All we need is time."

Jason Brolund, West Kelowna Fire Chief

Sunday morning, we headed out from Kokanee Springs Resort, loaded with a picnic cooler packed full of goodies fit for royalty. Several staff had lined up to wave goodbye, and we smiled back as we drove past. It was heartwarming.

But it was also time to leave. The Kootenays had felt like a refuge at first, but now had become a limbo of sorts. A place to wait and try to act ordinary, because life was normal for everybody around us in this idyllic summer golf resort. While elsewhere, waited the next circle of hell in Dante's Inferno.

Looking back, this sounds melodramatic, even to me. But, packing up on that first Sunday morning after being evacuated, we were sick and afraid. The wildfire had probably destroyed our home. And now we would be driving through West

Kelowna on our way to Peachland. Right past the exit to Westside Road. Past our neighbourhood.

When the news reporters announced that Task Force 1 had landed, I grimaced; thinking it all sounded very heroic and exciting for listeners who hadn't been affected by the McDougall Creek wildfire. But for us, it was ominous. The task force had a laser-focused agenda: making sure no one had been killed by the fire, and counting the damaged and burned properties.

It would be horrible to discover that someone (or more than one) had died in the fire. My mouth went dry thinking about it. But I willed myself to believe otherwise. In any case, now that Task force 1 was here to conduct the investigation, the suspense would soon be over.

Meaning that, among other things, we'd soon find out for sure if our house was gone.

I WAS on the phone with my daughter as we drove down the eerie, deserted highway. Now and then, Lorenzo ceased his constant nervous tapping of the steering wheel and glanced down at the sandwich I had placed beside him; ambivalent about whether to unwrap it and dig in. I loosened the saran wrap with my free hand and nudged him encouragingly.

"How are you doing?" Daria asked. Her neutral voice made smile fondly. I knew she didn't want to set me off.

"Ok. I mean...you know." I paused. "We're about twenty kilometres away from downtown. We'll pick up Oliver first and then swing by and say hi on the way through."

"Awesome. I'll put the coffee on." This casual remark almost made me break down. But I heard my five-month-old granddaughter's little warbles in the background and knew I needed to keep a rein on my emotions.

"Great!" I replied. "Coffee's just what we need. How's everything there?"

"Um." She paused. "It's very smoky here. Just saying. If you're not seeing it yet, be prepared."

We were on speaker phone. Lorenzo and I glanced at each other and peered out the window. Although still dim, the sky was blue, with no visible smoke.

"Thanks. See you soon." I ended the call, not wanting her to hear the tremor in my voice. We were silent for a moment. Lorenzo pushed his sandwich away. I thought of what we were driving toward, which would be nothing like we had driven away from two days ago. An eternity ago.

"God help us," I breathed.

Lorenzo didn't answer, but squeezed my arm, keeping his eyes straight ahead.

Sure enough, a few kilometres down the road, everything changed. The air became hazy, visible smoke drifting in the near distance. A smell of burning, though not like campfire smoke—more chemical than that—infiltrated through the window cracks.

Smoke choked the Okanagan

Soon afterward I learned that even when you *can* smell wildfire smoke, it doesn't smell good (like campfire smoke) because the atmosphere destroys all those delicious "S'mores-type-smells" first, leaving behind the nastier ones.

The second thing we saw was a bunch of water bombers overhead, the propellers droning as they went back and forth from the lake to the hillside. Helicopters, air tankers…the sky was busy. No wonder the airport was closed. My throat tightened again with that choking "it's-the-end-of-world-as-we-know-it" feeling.

Irrational? Not if you were there.

We drove into downtown Kelowna, straight to Okanagan Spirits, the shop where Oliver's dog sitter Lynn (a teacher at Okanagan College) works part-time in the summers, just for fun. The funky downtown store is situated nearby the strip of waterfront restaurants, and specializes in gin-tasting flights. Who wouldn't have fun there?

Oliver came bounding out to greet us, tongue lolling and eyes glowing. Lynn was right behind him. "He's become the store mascot," she declared, beaming like a proud parent. "People who come in here all worried about the fire are just rubbing him on the head like he's a statue of Buddha or something, and they instantly feel better. *He's* a little anxious, though..."

It was true, and very apparent. Oliver had wrapped himself around my ankles so tight I had to loosen his grip to take a step forward. He always missed us when we left, but this was obviously more than that just separation anxiety. He could doubtless sense the apprehension all around him. Now was the time to bring him back into the fold.

We thanked Lynn, packed Oliver in the overstuffed VW, and headed to Rutland to see family for the first time since the McDougall Creek wildfire swooped down like a marauding dragon and hurled us into limbo.

Much to my chagrin, as soon as I walked into my daughter's kitchen, I burst out crying. It was an embarrassing moment, and I pulled myself together as fast as I could. But there you have it. She didn't mind, but I did.

Unaware, Lorenzo shot the breeze with Sean in the living room, while Daria hugged me and patted my back until I gradually calmed down; after which she rewarded me by placing my cooing little granddaughter in my arms.

"How long are you staying in Peachland?" Daria asked,

offering a plate of blueberry muffins, then holding it out of reach as Maya tried to grab it with swift little velociraptor hands.

"Four days." I counted them out in my head. "Unless, you know…everything turns out to be fine with the house, in which case we can go home." My voice faltered, and into the silence came a little chortle in response.

We both looked at Maya, who was grinning at me with toothless joy, oblivious to the surrounding angst. I stroked her cheek, thinking there was nothing in this world as soft or resilient as a baby.

"Regardless of what's happening here," I continued, "we're going to the coast for a few days next week. Lorenzo has some overdue business meetings, and there are some people we want to see. Vicky and Tony offered us their place while they're in Europe—so nice of them. It'll feel way homier than an Airbnb."

"That's great!" Daria spoke cheerily. "By the time you're back, maybe all this will be in the rearview mirror…"

"Maybe."

In the living room, Lorenzo and Sean were chuckling about something. They were both handymen, so it probably involved power tools gone wrong. Their merriment was jarring. "How can they laugh like that?" I muttered, resting my cheek against Maya's downy little head for consolation.

"C'mon, Mom," Daria said. Her smile was wry. "Everyone has their own coping mechanisms. You should know."

We both knew. We'd lost my son Orion tragically fifteen years before. You cope however you can. And sometimes you don't.

I kissed Maya's cheek and handed her back to my daughter, who looked at me with undisguised concern. "No need to rush off."

"Yes there is. Maya needs to nurse soon and then sleep. Which means you should sleep, ha-ha. I remember those days. And there's no point in staving off the inevitable. It's better if we get to Peachland and settle in."

"So, are you going to be okay... driving through...?" She hesitated, appraising my reaction to her words.

The sentence hung unfinished. But the meaning was stark. When we walked out their door, we'd be driving through West Kelowna on our way to Peachland. Right past the exit that led to our home. There was no other route.

HEADING across the bridge from Kelowna to West Kelowna ignited a drumbeat of anxiety and fear that pulsed from my temples to my stomach, making me worry I might begin retching. I started to open the window but closed it again at Lorenzo's incredulous glance. He had a point. As we approached our neighbourhood, the air outside had become dense with smoke.

All at once, there was no more avoiding it. The Westside Road exit to Bear Creek was coming up. Until now, we had loved this turnoff, flipping on the right turn signal smugly every time, because we got to avoid all the backed-up traffic crawling along toward Westbank.

Now we were zooming up to the exit, and my nausea increased. I wanted to close my eyes, but the sight of the newly erected roadblock riveted me against my will. I sat bolt upright, my spine rigid and my nails digging into my palms, looking at the sign.

WESTSIDE ROAD CLOSED DUE TO WILDFIRE HAZARD! DO NOT ENTER!!

Even though we had steeled ourselves for the sight, the shock of it was like a kick in the teeth.

It was astounding. An outrage, in fact. How dare they keep us from our home? I began breathing faster, my breaths so shallow I was sure I'd hyper-ventilate. Lorenzo muttered a stream of barely audible profanities, some in Italian. We gazed at the impenetrable wall of smoke on the hillside above. Our neighbourhood. Our house. *Was it all gone...?*

Then, in a flash—like everything in life—the exit was behind us, and we were driving on.

After travelling down Highway 97 in gloomy silence for the next fifteen minutes, we saw the big orange peach standing atop a pole, right at Ponderosa, which was our signal to turn right. The Peachland peach—what a great landmark. How many people get to say: 'Just turn right at the giant peach!' when giving directions?

We'd been to Paula and Peter's place several times in the last couple of years, their beautiful home nestled near the top of winding Ponderosa Drive.

Moving to Kelowna during COVID-19 times had, of course, curtailed any chance to socialize in our new city. Being highly social, Paula and Peter had come up with a creative way to circumnavigate pandemic restrictions: the "Red Canoe" bar. They'd flipped their bright red canoe upside down and transformed it into a makeshift table, laying out trays of snacks and drinks for their frequent guests.

Along with other friends and neighbours, we'd looked forward to dropping by the Red Canoe for 'happy hour,' in a safe outdoor setting. Paula would play her guitar, Peter would tell stories of his rugby prowess in New Zealand, and we'd forget about scary viruses for a while.

Paula at the 'Red Canoe' bar in Peachland

After the COVID danger subsided, we had the pleasure of going to dinner parties inside their house, and they came to ours. Thinking back on those times reminded me how good life could be.

Now we were going there as evacuees to shelter from a wildfire. It was bizarre beyond imagining. But we were beginning to learn not to look too far beyond the next bend in the road.

10

PEACHLAND PONDERINGS

Winding up Ponderosa's steep hairpin curves, I had a brief moment of vertigo. It wasn't just the elevation. Okanagan Lake sparkled far below in the distance, silvery blue and ethereal. But smoky air and a hazy sky surrounded us, the incongruous contrast making me uneasy.

In the back seat, Oliver whimpered. Undeniably the most vocal dog I have ever encountered, and I have known my fair share. His repertoire included far more than just the standard growling and barking. Over the past eleven years, I learned the nuances of his language, the various pitches of sound that convey subtle emotions. (Dogs have evolved alongside us—how could they not become more complex?)

This whimper ended on an interrogatory note. *Why are we not going home? I have just come from the dog-sitters, where I have been a very good boy. We are supposed to be going home now...*

Oliver deserved a medal for being such a wonderful therapy dog

"I know." I reached back and scratched Oliver's ears. In normal times he goes into transports of ecstasy at this, but now he just fixed me with his one blue-eye-one-brown-eyed-gaze, reproachful. *You haven't answered my question.*

Fretting, I turned to Lorenzo. "He's probably even more freaked out because we were so tense going by the Westside Road exit."

"But we didn't even talk."

"Exactly. It's not like us. That's what's bothering him."

We were almost at the top of Ponderosa Drive. Such a beautiful spot, close to the iconic Pincushion Mountain hiking trailhead. But our dampened spirits diminished the beauty. And the smoky air persisted—even up this high—something I hadn't expected. It was a merciless reminder that the wildfire was close by, wreaking its ongoing havoc.

"There it is!" I'd spotted the red canoe, no longer overturned on stumps, but leaning against the shed, looking as if it had seen recent action in the lake. Paula's luscious summer dahlias were on display to the left of the front door, and I knew there would be more glorious floral parades in the back.

We stepped out of the car, stretching our cramped legs. It had been a long stretch of driving from Crawford Bay to Peachland. Released from the back seat, Oliver rushed up to the red canoe, barking a ferocious challenge, subsiding only when he realized inanimate objects don't fight back.

"Home, sweet home," I murmured. "Only it's not home."

Lorenzo put his arm around my waist and squeezed. "Stop dwelling on that. Think about how lucky we are."

"Yes." As we pushed through the door into the McLaughlin's spacious abode, I reminded myself we were in Peachland. Close to home, and in no personal danger.

Sometimes in a challenging situation, it's helpful to reflect upon how much worse things could be. We weren't fleeing a war-torn landscape, fearing for our lives. We hadn't lost any loved ones. I kissed Lorenzo's cheek, and then we took our bags and went through the door, Oliver padding close behind.

WE SETTLED back on the leather couch in the den, Lorenzo wielding the television remote like a light sabre as we turned on the news. Oliver stirred at our feet on the area rug, trying to accustom himself to more unfamiliar sights and smells.

After unpacking our bags, we'd ordered a pizza. Oliver got a special treat of slivered ham in his bowl of kibble. Tomorrow, we'd buy some groceries and prepare to hunker down for a few days.

Unless something changed, like the fire miraculously disappearing... and we got to go home. I tried without success to stop thinking this way.

The evening news began, focusing as usual on West Kelowna and the McDougall Creek wildfire. Fire Chief Jason Brolund appeared on the screen as this morning's news conference replayed. Fatigue lines were etched into his face. We leaned forward to listen.

Brolund stepped up to the microphone. "We're now four days in," he said. "It feels like months, but things are looking better. We haven't lost any homes in twenty-four hours."

This statement was greeted by a collective murmur of hope and excitement, but Fire Chief Brolund quelled any premature optimism with his next words. "There are still a million points of fire out there across our community." His voice was sombre. "It's far too soon to think about getting people back into their homes. Hang tight folks."

"But what about finding out which homes have burned, and which haven't?" I asked.

"Are you asking me, or TV Jason Brolund?" Lorenzo quipped, and I smacked him.

Still, the 'no houses in the last 24 hours' announcement contained a small piece of good news, and I clung to that scrap of hope.

AFTER WATCHING MORE wildfire coverage on the TV news channels for a while, we decided it was time to take a mental health break and watch a comedy. But by this time, it was apparent word of the fire had hit big time on an international level. Friends and family from all over—Italy, Germany, Norway—were bombarding us with enquiries. We'd run out of excuses not to respond to people, so it became a busy night of texting, emailing, and fielding phone calls.

Now it was close to midnight. "Time for bed," I announced, bleary-eyed. I turned off my phone and tossed it to the end of the couch like it was a volatile grenade. Lorenzo nodded and stood, yawning, then headed for the stairs down to the guest room.

Wandering through the kitchen, I stepped out onto the

balcony for a moment, wanting to enjoy the cool of the evening amid Paula's lovingly tended flower and herb baskets.

But the air was still dim, with scant visibility. No amount of squinting at the sky produced even the slightest glimmer of starlight or moonlight. Ash particulate hung like a pall, and even Paula's foliage looked limp and defeated.

I decided it was better inside than out. Turning out the lights, I went to bed, Oliver's furry cheek brushing my heels.

I had my first wildfire nightmare that night. It wouldn't be the last.

∽

TRIPWIRE NIGHTMARE

It was time to leave Peachland and go home. No word had come for days from anyone in Kelowna, including my daughter and son-in-law. I worried about them and baby Maya. In the dream, Lorenzo's youngest daughter Nicole also lived in Kelowna, and we were worried about them and our other baby granddaughter Lily.

Our cell phones emitted a weird buzz whenever we tried to use them. If we persisted, the sound got louder, accompanied by an ominous crackling.

Oliver was in the back yard out among the juniper hedges, out of sight but within earshot. It was time to put him in the car, so I called out to him. He emerged from the shrubbery instantly, but when I beckoned him further, he hesitated, stepping gingerly toward the lawn and coming to an abrupt halt, staring at me with panicked eyes.

Inside, I glimpsed Lorenzo shutting off the last of the lights in the house. He stepped out and locked the door, calling out for me. I sensed his impatience to leave. It matched mine.

We had to go. Now.

"Come!" I snapped my fingers at Oliver, irritated. He commenced a frantic skittering, trotting toward me and then retreating. He is the most obedient dog on the planet, so I shook my head in disbelief as I tried to coax him. This made no sense.

Then I saw them.

Crimson lines, slender as crosshairs, running across the perimeters of the lawn. I walked down the stairs of the back deck and stepped onto the grass, gazing down. Inches in front of my foot, a thin line glowed. Trying to ignore it, I stepped forward.

In an instant, a wall of flame flared up in front of me. Heat seared my face, and a burning smell arose. It was my hair being scorched from my head.

I leaped back.

Gasping, I staggered down the lawn a few feet and tried to flee in a different direction—toward the front of the house. But the red line was there too, between the lawn and the driveway, and stepping toward it, the flames flared at me in warning, daring me to cross that line. I sensed a malicious glee...

I opened my mouth to scream for Lorenzo. Behind me, Oliver whimpered from the bushes, but I couldn't reach him. At the same time, Lorenzo's shadow moved past me, his head bowed in defeat.

In the omniscient way of dreamers, I knew that if one of us moved beyond that line, we would trigger the 10,000-hectare fire to materialize at this location. We couldn't leave. We couldn't take a step beyond those crimson lines.

The fire had trapped us at last.

11

MORE BAD NEWS

Excerpt from *CBC News,* Monday August 21:
AT LEAST 50 WEST KELOWNA STRUCTURES LOST TO WILDFIRE, BUT WORST HIT AREAS YET TO BE SURVEYED

Premier David Eby and cabinet ministers to visit areas affected by fire on Tuesday.

*More help is on the way, as hundreds of firefighters from Mexico and South Africa are set to arrive.

*Smoke is blanketing much of the province, prompting air quality advisories and special weather statements.

*A provincewide state of emergency is in place in B.C.

*Non-essential travel to the southern interior has been restricted, as 27,000 people are under evacuation orders, about a third of them in the Kelowna area.

OUR NEXT DAY in Peachland was surreal and restless.

Surreal, because the poor air quality was beyond our wildest imaginings. The toxicity level measured at 11+. It doesn't get much higher than that. Authorities were advising residents to stay indoors unless there was dire necessity to go outside. If we absolutely had to, then we should wear a mask.

Restless, for the same reason. We couldn't even go for a walk, although our anxiety levels were off the charts. Of course Oliver still needed to go out, and we had plenty of masks, but five minutes of activity a couple of times a day didn't cut it for two active people.

I'm accustomed to teaching eight fitness classes a week, plus hiking and swimming during the warmer months. Lorenzo has also always been active—cycling, running, weight-training, playing racquet sports, and (you guessed it) golf. We weren't happy campers when we couldn't get some exercise, even at the best of times.

Stress made things worse. There had to be *some way* to move. I hit the jackpot when I stumbled across a couple of dumbbells and fitness bands in Paula's downstairs storage area. Devising a little workout circuit, and blasting a playlist of upbeat songs from my iPad made me feel a lot better. Lorenzo contented himself with sending out work emails, and then doing minor repairs around the house as part of our 'thank you' to our hosts.

Feeling a little more relaxed by that afternoon, we switched the TV on just in time to hear some terrible news that wiped out any vestige of tranquillity.

The McDougall Creek wildfire had obliterated Trader's Cove.

Trader's Cove was a quaint little lakeside community located just a short distance down Westside Road from where we lived. Hearing this news shocked and sickened us. We had driven to the area only a few weeks before, drawn back by the community's quaint vibe. Stopping in a little park to take some pics, I'd bumped into some bighorn sheep—beautiful, majestic, and as warily curious about me as I was about them.

The news report continued, becoming grimmer by the second. *Everyone* in Trader's Cove had lost their homes. *And us too*, went the refrain in my head. *Everything's gone.*

FINDING THE PHOENIX

The reporter was still speaking, and her next words made our heads snap up. *"And that's not all! Okanagan Lake Resort..."*

My memory of that day played on in my head. We had stopped in at Trader's Cove on the way home from a magical lakeside lunch at Okanagan Lake Resort. A longtime landmark along the rustic, gorgeous, stretch of Westside Road from Bear Creek to Fintry, the lakeside resort boasted a dock where pleasure crafts of various shapes and sizes pulled jauntily in and refuelled; their occupants grabbing tacos or burgers from the hip beach bar/cafe at Okanagan Lake Resort.

Okanagan Lake Resort pre-wildfire

Locals like us sat at the tables with our contented toes in the sand, sipping beer and watching the action, the bass-thumping pop music making everything seem even cooler.

Whenever we hung out at Okanagan Lake Resort, I felt like we were at a world-class watering hole in some exotic location. Come to think of it, we *were*. Oliver loved it too. He would find the best shade (often under a picnic table) and wait for us to drop crumbs from our chicken tacos.

The news reporter looked into the camera and told us the

horrifying news: Okanagan Lake Resort had burned to the ground.

Okanagan Lake Resort burning to the ground (Photo credit Les York/CBC)

Although she relayed this in a solemn tone, the news reporter's voice was somewhat detached, almost as if all the B.C. wildfire drama was getting repetitive. Yet on the TV screen behind, appalling footage of the burning resort underscored the magnitude of this escalating catastrophe. Flashes of my tripwire nightmare assailed me, sparking through my body like tiny electric shocks.

"Are you kidding me?" I clutched Lorenzo's arm, digging in my nails. He didn't flinch or try to pull away. "Is everything beautiful that we've found up here going to be burned to cinders?"

"I know." Lorenzo paused and put his arms around me. "That's what it feels like. It's hideous."

After that we ran out of words. We just sat together, staring into space. This nightmarish cycle of destruction just kept going. The McDougall Creek wildfire seemed insatiable, and unstoppable. A fervent desire washed over me, to just go lie under a blanket somewhere, and refuse to come out. I didn't want to know what would happen next.

12

ONE WEEK IN

Excerpt from *Castanet* **Newspaper,** Tuesday August 22
Premier David Eby flew into the Okanagan for a tour, where he saw the devastation firsthand.

"This is such an awful time for so many people. I want to reassure people that I find it unacceptable that any person has to wait to get into a hotel to get the support they've needed," the premier said during a news conference, while pledging provincial support in clearing the backlog of evacuees.

The public also learned more details of damage estimates when it was announced that approximately 190 homes were damaged or destroyed.

The smoke has finally lifted, giving residents a look at the destruction left behind by the fire.

Premier Eby speaks to media after helicopter tour of wildfire devastation (Photo Credit: B.C. Wildfire Service via Twitter)

It was Tuesday, August 22, and the wildfire had been burning for a week. It seemed more like a month. We ventured out for a walk along Peachland's waterfront to meet our other Peachland friends, Deb and Greg, for an early dinner at the popular lakeside Italian restaurant, Cibo and Vines.

They'd been in Vancouver when the wildfire changed the Okanagan's landscape, and were anxious to connect with us and make sure we were okay. *As if,* I wanted to say. But it would be a nice distraction to see friends, and I had been good friends with Deb since my Tsawwassen days. Plus, we'd been inside all day, and all three of us were like caged animals, with Oliver being the most civilized of the lot.

The smoky air clogged our throats, making our brisk walking pace feel like we were running a 10K. Other passersby seemed subdued, and the general atmosphere carried none of the usual height-of-summer lightheartedness. Oliver trailed behind a little way, sniffing at the surroundings with a suspicious air. Just like us, he wanted to be home.

I COULDN'T STOP THINKING about our next door neighbours. Chantelle and Tim had chosen the Hotel Eldorado to shelter in after their first couple of nights staying with friends in the city.

Like most other local hotels, the Eldorado had set aside blocks of their rooms for evacuees at a discounted rate. Insurance would cover the cost, so at least they had a roof over their heads. But they had so many challenges, it must be overwhelming. I texted her as Lorenzo and I ambled along Beach Avenue.

How's it going at the Eldorado?

It has a great swimming pool, Chantelle responded, within a scant ten seconds. **Nash is over the moon, because he's always after us about getting a pool.**

That's a good thing! If he's happy and distracted, you can breathe a sigh of relief.

Yup. He loves the restaurant too, because they have great fries. But now and then, he remembers about the fire—and asks about his goldfish. 😰😱

My stomach lurched. I had often wondered about the fire's impact on wildlife, and if any pets or livestock were trapped or left behind in the evacuation's panic.

What do you tell him? I ventured.

I can't tell him anything, because I don't know. But the odds aren't good for the fish. They've been in the extreme heat for days. So, I try and change the subject—ask him to do a cannonball into the pool or something…lol.

Lol.

After sending the reply, I rubbed my eyes, unable to stave off the image of Nash's playhouse burning… Poor Chantelle. Again, I couldn't imagine how I'd cope if I had young children to buffer from all of this unforeseen destruction.

The morning news had reported that, for the first time, the wildfire had showed no growth overnight. But by then it had grown to a staggering 12,000 hectares (almost 30,000 acres) in size. Fire crews remained on the scene and spokespeople for the BC Wildfire Service said that visibility was challenging because of the thick smoke, limiting the ability to get an updated aerial track. I re-read the post to Lorenzo as we walked.

"The smoke," Lorenzo remarked glumly. "That must be why there's still no information on which of our houses were destroyed." Adding, "And good luck to Sean and Pierre on that front..."

I shot him a mirthless grin. Just before we left for our walk, our neighbour Pierre and our son-in-law Sean had texted us separately with an identical idea—although they couldn't have cooked it up together, because they'd never met.

The idea was to use some high-powered binoculars and get up high, somewhere as close to our neighbourhood as possible, to see which homes were still standing.

If any.

Our son-in-law Sean had served (with distinction) in the Canadian Armed Forces for several years and already had a pair of military grade binoculars. Pierre had acquired some from who-knew-where. He and Colleen were returning to Kelowna in a few days to meet up with neighbours and commiserate.

A few minutes ago, Pierre had texted Lorenzo that a bunch of neighbours were going to get together at the hill beside Shopper's Drug Mart the day after tomorrow and try to get a view of our street. The winds were predicted to have cleared away much of the smoke by then.

"In his mind he's James Bond," Lorenzo grumbled, frowning. I thought I knew what was bugging him. We were driving to the coast in two days, so he wouldn't get to be part of the reconnaissance mission.

It was all at once easy to relate to Pierre and Colleen's ambivalence about returning to Edmonton. They had separated themselves from the pack.

The realization hit me that I was also discomfited at the prospect of going down to smokeless Tsawwassen; walking along the beach trail under a clear, untroubled sky, when our fellow evacuees were (literally) in the thick of things.

One part of me wanted to escape all this dreadful suspense—

not to mention the poisonous air. But another part had become rooted to our new community, as we all waited and hoped for things to get better. Being away from the others felt wrong, somehow. I tried to put my thoughts into words without seeming melodramatic.

"We should make some time to hang out with some of our neighbours before we go down to the coast." I looked at Lorenzo wistfully, waiting for a response. He was peering into his phone, no doubt answering a work-related question, and gave me an absent-minded nod.

"Why don't we zip over to Kelowna tomorrow and see if we can meet Chantelle and Tim for coffee or lunch?" I suggested. "They could use the moral support."

"That would be backtracking." Lorenzo muttered. He still seemed out of sorts. "It doesn't make sense to go all the way back to downtown Kelowna, does it? It was hard enough to drive by our exit yesterday. For a second I thought you were going to throw yourself out of the car and become roadkill."

This attempt at black humour was out of character for him—that was *my* department, and it didn't sit well. I couldn't help snapping back. "*Nothing* about this makes sense. What's your point?"

We stared at each other, suddenly bristling and at odds. Oliver gave an alarmed little yip, and I leaned down and ruffled his head.

Just then, an unexpected breeze came up, bringing a welcome bit of freshness. And we spotted Deb and Greg waving to us from the doorway at Cibo & Vines.

We lifted our hands at the exact same time to wave back, and then grinned at each other. Our moods picked up. "Let's talk about it later," Lorenzo said.

I was fine with that.

Having a brief reprieve with Peachland friends Deb and Greg

But our life was back *there*, in West Kelowna, and our future was intertwined with that of our Royal Heights neighbours. The connection tugged at me like an invisible magnet.

13

A RAY OF LIGHT

Wednesday morning dawned a little clearer. The air quality alert had dropped to "8," still very high, but we decided it was worthwhile risking a walk along the trail at the end of Ponderosa Drive. Oliver was ecstatic at this development. He immediately began chasing chipmunks, some real and some a figment of his imagination.

Our phones buzzed simultaneously. My text came from Chantelle and Lorenzo's from Dan, both with the same message. Lorenzo read his message aloud, his eyes gleaming with excitement.

"Dan says there's aerial footage of our street on Facebook! It's not official, just some guy flying a private helicopter over our neighbourhood. Apparently some of the houses are visible through the smoke. He's sending me the link!"

Chantelle's text began with: **OMG, OMG, OMG!!!** It also contained a link to the post.

The video was unsanctioned, and its source was unknown, but this footage was all we had to go on. We began searching our phones with trembling hands.

"Wait," Lorenzo said, "let's just go back to the house and

watch it on the laptop." That made sense, and we turned off the hiking trail and hightailed it back to Peter and Paula's place.

Without bothering to sit down, I grabbed my Mac, plunked it on the kitchen counter, and opened Facebook.

And there it was: an eighteen-second clip from an independent chopper pilot. Staring at the barely discernible outlines of our neighbourhood from far above made my head spin and my eyes burn. It was almost as if the viscous smoke captured on camera was seeping from the computer screen.

Chopper footage of our neighbourhood

"Where are *we*?" I asked Lorenzo, hearing the whine in my voice but unable to suppress it. "*Where's our house?*"

Geography has never been my strong suit, and seeing my neighbourhood from a camera on a helicopter through a blur of turbulence and smoke did nothing to improve my vision or orientation skills.

Lorenzo squinted. It wasn't easy for him either, I observed with grim satisfaction. Although he was the opposite of me—if he had been an Italian Captain Bly, he could have spotted Tahiti from the deck of the Bounty, without a telescope, while staving off a mutiny.

Lorenzo ignored my griping; hitting pause and rewind several times as he tried to get his bearings.

"Oh, no!" he exclaimed suddenly, pointing. I peered at where his finger had landed. Confused. All I saw was a huge mound of what looked like junk.

"What *is* that?"

"It's just past the gate," Lorenzo said grimly. "Don't you see? That *used* to be House #1. It's burned. It's gone."

I gaped. *Mariko's house?*

Mariko's home was the first house past the Royal Heights gate when you drove through, at the bottom of the "V" of the two-pronged cul-de-sac. Her house is on the left side of the street, at the bottom. Ours was also on the left side, three houses from the top.

"What about the house next to Mariko's?"

House #2 belonged to Mike and Mo. I didn't know them well, just that they were a pleasant young couple. Neighbourhood buzz had it that Mo had just found out they were pregnant with their first child.

We watched, then Lorenzo paused the video. "Mike and Mo's house is gone," he said, throat hoarse with emotion. "Look, there's almost nothing left, just a big smoking pit."

"I can't believe this." A moan escaped me. The camera was moving so fast. My head spun. "Can you stop and rewind it?" I asked Lorenzo. He shook his head, and I grasped his urgency. *Let's get to our house…*

I peered closer as Lorenzo traced his finger along the path of the street. He hit 'pause'. "There's Pierre and Colleen's place!" he exclaimed. "Still there…"

Warmth flooded me. Their beautiful home, still standing. Hope, hope, hope…until the realization hit: Colleen and Pierre's place was House #3, next to the two that were burned to the ground. How could that be possible? The sinking realization deepened as the chopper kept going. We had just seen houses standing and houses burned, right beside each other. There was no way of knowing about ours until we actually saw it.

Lorenzo pressed 'play' again, then reared back, clapping his hands together. "That's Tim and Chantelle's place!" he exclaimed. "It's standing!" I hooted with jubilation.

Our house was next. The helicopter flew toward it as I gazed, paralyzed with suspense. Hearts hammering, we looked for our house through the smoke.

Then "It's there!" Lorenzo squeezed my shoulder... "Our house!" He pressed pause and froze the footage right above our home.

And there it was...I could see the deck and the roof, but little else, because the helicopter had been flying quite high.

We held hands and started hopping up and down in place, springing off the balls of our feet. "Oh my God!" I kept yelling.

Oliver began barking in a panicked way, not sure if we were happy or distraught. I petted him absent-mindedly, not taking my eyes off the screen. We watched the video again, then once more, gradually calming down. As sanity returned, we stopped jumping for joy.

I squinted in concentration. Where were the hydrangea bushes? The entire front garden landscaping seemed to have vanished. My stomach clenched as I glimpsed several glowing spots through the smoke. "What are those things?" I asked, gulping. "Those red things? Are they spot fires?"

Lorenzo leaned forward to look. "I don't think so..." But he sounded hesitant.

Just then, his phone buzzed, and I heard Pierre's booming voice. Lorenzo put the phone on speaker. "Are you guys looking at the video?"

"Yes," Lorenzo replied.

"Then you see our houses are still there, right?" His exultance spilled out of the phone speaker, and we smiled indulgently. Then I nudged Lorenzo.

"Judith's worried about the red glowing areas, though," Lorenzo said. I looked at him. *"We're* worried about them," he amended. It was a relief to have him drop the 'Man of Steel' act.

"Just a sec." For moment, Pierre sounded concerned. Then he started chuckling. "Those are siren lights! There's a fire truck in front of your place. They must be keeping an eye on things, maybe putting out spot fires. Thank God for those guys!"

"Yes! Thank God for them..." My gratitude to the firefighters reached a new level. I was vibrating from head to toe.

Our house was still there.

Chantelle phoned me just then, and we had a brief conversation that consisted mainly of joyous shrieking. And even though my voice was hoarse for a couple of days after, the cathartic shouting was worth every second. It's always good to have a shriek buddy, in my opinion.

And it's good to have some light in the darkness, even if it's the siren glow of a fire truck through a thick blanket of smoke.

14

POISONED JOY

Excerpt from *Castanet* **Newspaper**, Wednesday August 23, 2023

    For the first time in days, the McDougall Creek wildfire was visible overnight from the valley below. The smoke cleared Tuesday, revealing the devastation left behind by the still out-of-control wildfire.- Central Okanagan Emergency Operations did not rescind any evacuation orders or alerts.

Gripped by compulsion, Lorenzo and I replayed the helicopter footage over and over again. Pierre and Sean had also independently taken some pics with their binoculars, so over the next couple of days we studied those too, until our eyes watered.

We were so relieved to see Raj and Sutha's place still there, and also Dan and Mariana's home standing next door to us on the other side.

But with each video replay, our dismay grew at the sight of gaping spots and piles of junk where many of our neighbours' houses had once stood.

Steve and Tracy's across the street. Aleda and Joseph's place at the top of the hill, two houses north of us. Mike and Mo's, House #2, next to Pierre and Colleen's place.

On the lower cul-de-sac it looked even worse. House after

house incinerated. One of those, House 32, belonged to a young couple from Eastern Canada named Seagun and Cory Laboucane. They were shucking oysters when the evacuation order came, and didn't take it seriously so kept on shucking until the police showed up at their door.

They had to flee their home, collect their two foster children, and find out their home was burned to the ground, while feeding the kids in a Spaghetti Factory on their way to the coast. (Fast forward: They ended up staying in *sixteen* different places throughout their evacuation).

Burned house on our street, Bear Creek Road

Seeing the widespread destruction in our beautiful neighbourhood was like watching a horror movie. Instead of being able to rejoice wholeheartedly at the sight of our home still standing, I drifted over to the couch and collapsed in a heap, staring morosely up at the ceiling.

Closing my eyes, I could see the billowing cloud of smoke surrounding our neighbourhood, swathing it in grief and uncertainty. Even Oliver's paw on my shoulder didn't comfort me. His velvety nose nuzzled my chin, and I relented a little and scratched his ears, thinking he would normally have hopped up beside me, but didn't dare, because it wasn't *his* couch.

It felt like we'd been displaced for a hundred years.

As the day wore on, I roused myself from my depressed slump. Lorenzo and I soldiered on with our various tasks, but the rest of the day went by in a kind of stupour. That initial burst of euphoria had been infiltrated by a simmering frustration, mingled with dread.

We couldn't go home. This wasn't over. The fire was still active, even on our street. Besides, no one knew what damage our homes had incurred. The front landscaping was gone. What about the roof? What about...?

As if reading my mind, around dinnertime Chantelle sent me a screen shot of their house, taken from the aerial footage.

Do you see that black thing at the back of our house?
What black thing?
Look closer.

I peered again at the hazy picture. Sure enough, a dark spot smudged the back of their house like a sooty thumbprint.

I see it.
What do you think it is?
I assume it's just a shadow. The angle of light...?
Hmmm. It's bugging me.
Try not to let it bug you. There's enough to worry about...
True. WOW, what a day it's been! CONGRATS TO US. But I feel so bad for everyone who... well, you know. Gotta get Nash to bed. TTYL.

I LAY awake in the darkness, listening to Lorenzo's rhythmic breaths on one side of me and Oliver's gentle snores from his dog bed on the other side.

It was impossible to harness the jumble of emotions surging through me. One minute I was elated at the knowledge that our home was still standing. I loved that place more than anywhere I'd ever lived. Maybe, now that the fire was gone from our neighbourhood, I'd soon be home, chopping veggies in the kitchen and looking at the sparkling blue lake...

The next moment sorrow engulfed me at the memory seeing our neighbours' incinerated homes in that helicopter video. All the anticipatory mourning I'd carried with me for days had become inescapable reality for them. Even if we could go home soon, things wouldn't be the same. Tears seeped from my eyelids.

Nothing would ever be the same.

This tumultuous roller coaster of conflicting thoughts continued to bombard me for several hours until I thought I'd scream. *I'll probably have terrible nightmares tonight*, I thought gloomily, just before falling into a dreamless slumber that lasted the rest of the night.

15

THE FISHING EXPEDITION

Turned out my argument with Lorenzo about going back to Kelowna to meet Tim and Chantelle had been unnecessary. A text from Chantelle the next morning decided the point.

We've got some news about our house. Are you guys around to meet up?

It took us only half an hour to drive from Peachland back to downtown Kelowna. This time, we averted our eyes from the blockade sign for the Westside Road exit.

Hotel Eldorado is picturesque, situated on Lakeshore Drive at the southern end of Pandosy Street. It sits right on the water at scenic Gyro Beach, boasting a wooden pier walkway and boat dock, along with the trendy and popular restaurant *Maestro*.

Which is where we met Chantelle and Tim, while their best friends supervised Nash at the pool, and another friend dog-sat Oliver and Jax in the hotel room, The two pooches were happy to reunite—they'd become 'best buds' from the moment they met two years ago.

Before launching in, we all ordered beers by unspoken accord, although none of us are typical lunch-time drinkers. A wiry young server with smoothly gelled hair brought it in record time. He flashed a friendly smile before gliding away.

"Cheers!" said Tim, in his laid-back laconic fashion, raising his beer. "Here's to houses that aren't burnt to the ground." We all clinked glasses. I could think of more uplifting toasts, truth be told.

"What's your news?" Knowing my voice sounded tense, I tried to relax my features into a smile.

"First, how are you guys? You've been flying all over the place like you're pinball wizards. Coping ok?" Chantelle had reverted to her role as a mental health care professional. It was sweet, but I was too worried to waste time on small talk.

"We're fine. And you're too young to even know what pinball is." I drummed my fingers on the table. "Now what about your house?"

You'll have guessed my question was not entirely disinterested. Their house is next door to ours. The fates of our homes were intertwined.

"Well..." She glanced at Tim, who rolled his eyes and took a quick gulp of his IPA. "You remember I was talking about Nash's goldfish?"

"Yes." I winced, thinking again of all the possibly endangered pets. Lorenzo leaned forward to listen.

"Well, hark back to this screenshot of the back of our house I sent you last night—*you've* seen it, right?" She turned to Lorenzo, brandishing her phone, and he gave her a cautious nod.

"Like I said, it was bugging me like crazy, because there's no way we can get in to see our neighbourhood and find out. It's too dangerous. Really bummed about that, needless to say. But then, by fluke, I went into the ESS center last night to get Jax some food, and everything fell into place..."

Chantelle's story had some unquestionable hijinks and espionage. Not surprising, if you know her. She thinks fast on her feet, and it doesn't take much for her street smarts to kick into full gear.

Like many evacuees, their family had registered at the hastily organized ESS centre to assist evacuees. Chatting with the pet support worker, Chantelle discovered something that was a game changer. Although *we* couldn't access our neighbourhood, designated professionals could enter as needed, like firefighters and police officers. *Duh*, you're saying, but—wait for it—also pet rescue workers.

Hearing this, Chantelle wondered aloud, her voice quavering, about the welfare of their beloved goldfish, about whom everyone in the family was worried sick. Could someone please go find out how the little buggers were doing? If possible, even rescue them?

Now I'm not saying Chantelle wasn't worried about the fish. (Nash, if you're reading this at a later date, I hope you've gained context and perspective). But she didn't hold out much hope for them under the circumstances.

What she wanted was to find out about their *house*. So, she put in her request, and the lovely pet support worker got official clearance to go on a goldfish rescue mission. She set off to on her quest that very morning, to Royal Heights Properties, 1525 Bear Creek Road, House #6.

A fishing expedition, if you will.

After Chantelle related this first part of the story, she took a sip of beer. Lorenzo chuckled at her ingenuity, and I broke into spontaneous applause.

Chantelle had been looking triumphant, but now her expression changed, and she fell silent, eyes downcast. Tim shifted in his chair, looking out the window at the pier.

"Well," I prompted, "Have you heard from her yet?"

"Yup," she said in a more subdued voice. "She called me within a couple of hours with her intel."

It was not good news.

The volunteer had arrived at their house and discovered broken glass littering the ground, a smashed-in front door, and caution tape surrounding the property. She sought information from firefighters who were patrolling the neighbourhood. They told her the interior of the house was largely destroyed.

When the stunned pet support worker enquired about the goldfish (I can only picture the look on the firefighters' faces) she was gently told that not only were the fish gone, but also the room they had resided in: Nash's bedroom. All ravaged by the blaze.

The outside structure still stood only because the firefighters had crashed through the door with axes and put out the fire. Oh, and also the water-bombing aircraft from above.

Whether the foundation was sound remained to be seen, but their home as they knew it was no more.

THAT BLACK SPOT Chantelle glimpsed on the helicopter video was, in fact, an immense hole—the disintegrated wall crumpled around it. She'd been right to be worried.

We sat there, dazed.

"Are you okay?" I whispered, after a few minutes of everyone sipping their beer and staring out at the lake with welling eyes. "I don't mean okay…but…"

Chantelle waved her hand. "I had a feeling. The black spot looked to me like a gaping hole. I had to find out if what I feared was true." She paused. "It's better to know, right?" Tim rubbed his forehead with his fingers, saying nothing.

"One day at a time." This from Lorenzo. He patted her hand gingerly, as if it was made of glass. We all murmured our agreement. Sometimes the biggest cliches are the greatest truths.

Looking back now, I admire Tim and Chantelle's composure at such a fraught moment in their lives, when they must have been struggling to cope. And I'm honoured we had gained their trust enough for them to confide in us.

Just then, our server with the slicked-back hair sidled up and dropped a bill down on our table for exactly zero. When we exclaimed and protested, he held up his hand for silence. "We're just hoping you folks can all go home soon," he said with a sympathetic smile. When I looked at him, his eyes were suspiciously wet.

People in this town felt deeply about what was going on, and knew. how to take care of their own. Another step towards my Finding the Phoenix.

We walked back in subdued silence to collect Oliver.

Firefighters' axes shattered the glass in Chantelle's front door to put out the inside fire

Pandemonium reigned in the hotel room where the kids were having a Nerf Gun war. Oliver and Jax were chasing each other around, playing tug-of-war with a stuffed moose, while Chantelle's friend Tara giggled at their antics.

"At least the pups had a good time," Chantelle joked, when we hugged goodbye. But as she turned away, her eyes shoulders slumped, and my heart sank.

They had a long road ahead of them.

16

HOME IS WHERE THE HEART IS?

Excerpt from *Castanet* Newspaper, August 23, 2023

The Emergency Operations Centre will be launching a website later this week to inform property owners of damages.

Thousands of evacuees across the Central Okanagan remain anxious to learn about the fate of their homes, and later Wednesday, a new website is expected to come online where that information will be available.

Sally Ginter, the CAO of the Regional District of the Central Okanagan (RDCO) said in a perfect world, she would have preferred to have RDCO staff have personal calls with every resident who lost a home to the fire, but given the number of losses, the website was the most efficient option to get the information out quickly.

"The No. 1 burning question evacuees have is 'Do I have a home?' And we want to be able to get that information to them as quickly as possible," Ginter said.

～

WE WERE GEARING up to drive to Tsawwassen on Wednesday, where Lorenzo would attend some business meetings in Vancouver, and we could have some long overdue visits with friends and family.

I had planned a book signing of *Mirror of the Sea*, the second novel in my epic fantasy series; but I cancelled it, being too disheartened to contemplate any beaming smiles or glad-handing.

As mentioned, our friends Vicky and Tony had offered their home while they visited their son and his family in Norway. Lorenzo and I had sighed with relief and gratitude when they sent the text from the airport. Vicky was lucky she was already hours away, out of my clutches, or I would have given her an embarrassingly long hug.

This would be our fourth move since being evacuated. And, the way things were going, we still might not be able to go home after returning from the coast.

Planning for the worst, we had lined up yet another accommodation, with our good friends Jay and Jeanette, whose home is near ours, but on the other side of Highway 97 just around the corner from Quail's Gate winery. They'd offered us shelter previously, and next week they'd be away in Vancouver, so we'd have their place to ourselves should we need it.

What did we do to deserve such wonderful friends? I didn't know, and I decided not to overthink it. Just to appreciate the support and accept the helping hands being offered at a time such as this.

Naively, we had hoped to be home before now, but that dream had gone up in smoke (pun intended). But although disappointment and dread were often our reigning emotions, something else had begun to prevail: recognizing how fortunate we were being able to rely on friends and family.

Many other evacuees were on shakier ground, and the evacuation support system trying to help these victims was flailing, overwhelmed by this sudden and massive disaster.

More on that later. Now it was almost time to leave Peachland. I was glad we'd met up with Chantelle and Tim, although we wished we could've seen our other neighbours. *Such is the life of a gypsy,* I told myself.

Not wanting to bring it up at our distraught lunch, I'd texted Chantelle the next morning to ask if the pet support worker had mentioned anything about our house. Chantelle said she'd asked, but the volunteer said 'no', because she was just there to focus on *their* house and the goldfish situation.

But the pet support worker had gone on to say that it was shocking to see many of the houses on our street were gone, haphazard piles of ash and stone and metal all that remained. And the smoke was so thick they had to wear masks, which was tough because she had begun to cry for all the people who'd lost their homes, and tears were raining down her face throughout the short time she was there.

Fair enough. *Poor girl.* But disappointing, because we still didn't know how bad the damage to our house was. What if the wildfire had destroyed *our* interior?

Poor us, too, I thought, with a stab of self-pity.

She acted almost apologetic, Chantelle had texted. **Like it was somehow her fault, or that I might 'shoot the messenger'...**

News sources soon confirmed the pet support worker's report about the state of our neighbourhood.

"It's still very dangerous in the hardest hit areas like West Kelowna Estates," a local radio station reporter warned, as we drove back to Peachland. *"Power lines are down, there are gas lines leaking everywhere...Safe to say the residents of those areas cannot go back until the firefighters remove the hazards."*

Lorenzo reached over and flicked the radio to a music station, saying gruffly that we didn't need to hear anymore. He was right. Listening to these repetitive messages was demoralizing. We'd already received the message, loud and clear: we weren't going home anytime soon.

Seeing the devastation on our street was so traumatic

At least there was a snippet of good news: the smoke had partially lifted today for the first time. Back in Peachland, we ate an early dinner and scoured the news outlets for messages of hope. *Were we turning a corner?*

But all we saw were multiple scenes of destruction wreaked by the wildfire, each worse than the last.

Wrung out by the ghastliness of it all, we tried to switch our mindset. Lorenzo phoned his daughter Nicole and caught up on how they were doing as novice parents. Newborn granddaughter Lily was two months old, and the little family had visited us in Kelowna last week right before the fire struck. It seemed impossible now. How could it have been only last week?

Lorenzo and Nicole and I with baby Lily

I began emailing my fitness peeps in Tsawwassen.

This fit and fun group had been doing Zoom fitness classes with me throughout the pandemic—after our local gym shut down—and then we continued our online workouts after I moved to Kelowna. During the lockdown, we had dubbed ourselves *"The Bandits,"* in part because we used bands in a lot of our classes, but also because we felt like a roving band during COVID times.

Every time I visited the coast, *the Bandits* made a point of trying to meet for coffee, whether it was two of us or ten of us. We'd been through the pandemic together, and we had a tacit understanding that we would help each other weather the inevitable storms that life brought. This would be no exception and, although a little anxious, I was looking forward to it.

My only worry was I didn't want to get over-emotional about the wildfire situation. I told myself it was okay—I would be among friends. Some of these women had been doing fitness classes with me for over thirty years, back to when my kids were little. We went back a long way.

"At least four of them can make it for coffee," I told Lorenzo as we crawled under the covers. "It'll be so good to see everyone. I only hope I don't burst out crying when I walk through the door of the coffee shop."

"Just picture them all in their underwear," Lorenzo offered, in probably the most bizarre and unhelpful suggestion he'd made since the evacuation began.

~

Lying in bed with the lights off, I thought about the tumultuous last twenty-four hours. Visions of displaced animals kept cropping up. Goldfish, dogs, deer, bear, and all the other creatures, pet and livestock that depended on people; but also wildlife that lived free but had to battle the elements every hour of every day.

I suddenly recalled the day of evacuation, when my little stellar blue jay friend came to see me a few hours before that apocalyptic orange and grey funnel of smoke and fire appeared over the Rose Valley ridge.

Had Stella been trying to warn me? Or saying farewell?

What had happened to Stella? I wondered. And all the other animals, domestic and wild? Humans weren't the only ones suffering in this catastrophe.

17

BROKEN RAIL RANCH

Months after the calamitous wildfire ordeal, I was in my favourite Westbank nail salon, Revive Nails, and my charming nail technician, Tiffany, asked me whether I had enjoyed my summer. I told her about being evacuated from Royal Heights by the wildfire, and she gasped.

The customer beside me cleared her throat. "I'm Keramia Lawrie," she announced. I stared. The name sounded familiar. She gave me a sad smile. "From Broken Rail Ranch. We lived close by. I know how you feel."

Excerpt from *Kamloops Now* newspaper, August 18, 2023

IT'S GONE. BROKEN RAIL RANCH IN WEST KELOWNA DESTROYED BY THE MCDOUGALL CREEK WILDFIRE. MOST ANIMALS ABLE TO ESCAPE DANGER.

The Broken Rail Ranch in West Kelowna is gone. The iconic ranch, located on Petterson Road near Bear Creek Provincial Park, served as a hobby farm, animal rescue sanctuary, and offered guided trail rides through the stunning back country vistas of West Kelowna. Owners Jeff and Crystal Findlay shared on Instagram late last night that the property was engulfed and destroyed by the McDougall Creek Wildfire.

Instagram Post by Crystal and Jeff Findlay:

Our home and ranch are gone. Thank you to the first responders and police who tried their best...We are okay. Our horses and almost all our animals are okay. It's all about insurance now...

Here was more dire news, hitting me hard because it was so close to home—right up the street. Renowned for their humane treatment of animals, Broken Rail ranch owners Crystal and Jeff Findlay saved twelve horses from slaughter over the years. Broken Rail was a West Kelowna legend, and the community was heartbroken to hear about their tragedy.

However, this also turned out to be a 'Finding the Phoenix' moment. Astoundingly, in the short time they had to make their escape, the owners managed to save most of their livestock: nineteen horses, a miniature pony, two bunnies, four goats, two dogs, and four cats. Unfortunately, they couldn't coax their two 350 lb sister-pigs to go on the flatbed truck, so they had no choice but to leave them behind—giving them up for gone.

But the beloved pig 'Miss Pumba' was more of a survivor than anyone realized...

Pumba the Pig being fed by West Kelowna firefighters (Photo credit: Castanet Newspaper)

Excerpt from *CBC News*, **August 23, 2023**

Although the ranch was engulfed in flames last Thursday, Pumba was spotted by a helicopter roaming on the last patch of live grass on the property, said West Kelowna resident Keramia Lawrie, whose parents own the property.

"It's just a miracle," said Lawrie. "She was kind of in the eye of the storm, and she was unharmed. I mean, it's just crazy that she survived, not just because of the fire itself, but because of the heat and smoke!"

Lawrie said her father Jeff Findlay had tried to load Pumba and her sister pig Miss Wilbour for evacuation as the McDougall Creek wildfire advanced on the property last week. But the pigs were too frightened and stubborn, and Findlay had to leave without them, doing so while surrounded by flames that were cresting the hill.

The next few days were a whirlwind of emotions for the family as they worried about the fate of their beloved animals. "We really assumed they were both dead, because, as you know, the whole property was reduced to rubble," said Lawrie.

It wasn't until Sunday that they heard that Pumba was still alive. The 300 lb pet was spotted by a helicopter pilot in the middle of destroyed buildings and ashes. A sign of hope amidst heartbreak and devastation...

"The pilot actually threw down some granola bars from the helicopter, and then the next day we knew she was ok, and also the fires calmed down a bit," said Lawrie.

Sadly, Miss Wilbour was found dead on Monday.

The firefighters have been sending Lawrie photos of Pumba, who she said seems happy. She said the loss of Miss Wilbour left them brokenhearted...recalling the sounds she made when she was scratched. She also stated that a vet had checked on Pumba, who was doing well, and the family was looking forward to a reunion with their pet soon.

Lawrie said her parents, who are now staying in a hotel, are still processing the loss of their business and home. But she shared in an Instagram post that Miss Pumba the pig was a 'symbol of survival and hope.' "She's just as happy as can be—rooting around in the grass... She's got all this room to herself. She's just living her best life!"

The Okanagan resident has started a fundraiser to help her parents recover from the farm burning down and says the community has supported them in the aftermath of the devastating wildfire.

Every picture, and post, and news story that I saw about Miss Pumba brought a smile to my face; offering glimmers of light that helped stave off despair during those weeks of being evacuated, especially the first terrible days when we didn't know whether our house was still standing.

The Broken Rail livestock were fortunate they had human caretakers looking out for them. Not so with unlucky wildlife caught in the firestorm. No one knows how many wild animals perished in the fire; from the blaze itself, or from heat, smoke, dehydration or starvation. I remember seeing an emaciated-looking bear and distraught young fawns separated from their mothers. And, like the raven I'd encountered in the Kootenays, many birds looked sooty, dazed, and bedraggled.

However, other stories of wildlife perseverance and resilience soon emerged. Take the Bighorn Sheep, for instance.

Excerpt from *Castanet* Newspaper, August 25, 2023:

Some of the magnificent Bighorn Sheep of Westside Road survived the wildfire

The herd of Bighorn Sheep that frequent Westside Road appear to have survived the firestorm that claimed homes and wiped out much of the forest on the west side of Okanagan Lake.

In a photo shared by a volunteer working on Westside Road, the sheep can be seen lounging near the gates of Bear Creek Park, after what must have been a horrific ordeal.

The woman (who asked not to be named) saw the herd resting together, and then further along, there was an ewe with three kids (babies).

We loved those sheep, and had seen them countless times on our way to a hike at Bear Creek Park; or for a beer and a fish taco at Okanagan Lake Resort. On one occasion, we braked—along with a long line of other motorists—while a herd sauntered across the road. Beaming construction workers halted traffic to give the sheep the right of way.

Bighorn sheep demanding that traffic yield

It was an unforgettable moment. All of us humans, in cars or outside in hard hats, watched in awe as these magnificent creatures crossed Westside Road, walking past us with regal, dismissive glances. They then scaled sheer walls of rock and boulders in seemingly impossible feats of gymnastics. Like a walk in the park.

We already knew two rams from that herd died in the wildfire. Hearing that, I had cried. But now we knew the other sheep had survived.

The yin and yang of wildlife news continued during the days that followed. A black bear cub was found injured and had to be euthanized. The thought was almost unbearably sad. But the wildlife officers had also rescued its sibling, whom they said would probably recover.

Some months after the wildfire, I had the honour of speaking at length with Chief Robert Louie of the Westbank First Nation, on whose land we reside. We commiserated about the toll it had taken on the Westbank First Nation Reserves, as well as residents of leased land in the same general area—including our Royal Heights Properties on Bear Creek Road. And how it could have been much, much, worse.

I asked Chief Robert Louie about the Sylix people's spiritual perspective on the horrific natural disaster we had experienced. He paused, looking thoughtful, and then told me that the tribe's connection to the surrounding wildlife is a deep and sacred thing, and one of the most painful aspects of the wildfire was witnessing or imagining the toll it took on the beautiful animals of the Okanagan.

Okanagan bear cub suffering wildfire burns

Struggles. Defeat. Survival. I became ever more grateful that not one person had thus far succumbed to the fire.

A few weeks later, I heard an interview with a B.C. conservation officer about the long and short-term impact of wildfires on the environment. It was pretty interesting stuff. Asked to comment on our specific wildfire, he said, "The McDougall Creek Wildfire certainly led to the temporary displacement of wildlife. However, if the animals can make it through a wildfire season, the long-term results can be beneficial."

He explained that although at first discombobulated by a fire, wild animals often thrive once they get their bearings. New foliage springs up, richer than before, grass and shrubs and berries in great quantity, boosting their food source and enriching their environment.

Finding the Phoenix.

18

THE ENVELOPE, PLEASE...

Excerpt from *CBC* **News**, Tuesday August 22, 2023:
181 PROPERTIES CONFIRMED DAMAGED OR DESTROYED BY WILDFIRES IN B.C.'S OKANAGAN REGION

Officials urge patience as they work to make neighbourhoods safe for residents to return.

∽

ON WEDNESDAY, August 23, we were still in Peachland, trapped indoors by the persistent smoke-poisoned air. We were readying ourselves to leave for Tsawwassen the next day. I sorted through laundry in a half-hearted way, trying to ignore Lorenzo's restless pacing as he prowled beside the kitchen windows overlooking the balcony. It was driving me crazy.

I turned the TV on to catch the noon news hour. Naturally West Kelowna's state of emergency was the top story. My head whipped up as the newscaster announced the municipality had launched the website they'd been talking about—enabling wildfire evacuees to find out the status of their properties.

Lorenzo stopped pacing and rushed to his laptop on the

kitchen counter. I dropped a pile of clothes back into the basket and bolted to look over his shoulder.

Clicking on the website, we saw a long list of properties, some on Bear Creek Road. My heart leapt every time I saw our street on the list. But Royal Heights wasn't among them, and I exhaled through a throat thick with disappointment.

The uncertainty was wearing me down. "I don't know how much longer I can take this," I told Lorenzo in a grim voice, and slumped off to put away the laundry. I vented my frustration by tossing half-folded clothes around the bed and mumbling profanities. Oliver sidled up to me and nudged me with his nose, making an empathetic sound in the back of his throat. This had been happening a lot in recent days.

Eventually my curiosity go the better of me; and soon I was peering over Lorenzo's shoulder again; dazed at the sheer number of properties.

There were hundreds of addresses, divided into three categories: "Total loss," "No major structural damage," and "Structural damage observed." The wording was stark—no sugarcoating here.

"Can you imagine?" I mused. "Finding out your house has burned down by seeing the words 'Total loss' on the list?"

We shuddered at the thought. Knowing from the helicopter video that our house was still standing was a partial consolation. But what if it was a burned-out shell, like Tim and Chantelle's house? It was driving me crazy not to know.

"It won't be long now," Lorenzo assured me, "probably by tomorrow, I'm thinking." But he didn't sound convinced.

That afternoon Fire Chief Brolund held another press conference, in which he informed us the winds had shifted and the dense wildfire smoke that had shrouded the mountains was lifting.

"We haven't seen the landscape since the fire," he warned, his earnest, boyish face reminding me of someone's worried older brother, "and it's going to look very…different. And it might be pretty dramatic to see what we have lost."

He paused, then added, "I know lots of you are tired. Tired of being out of your homes. Tired of this situation—and so are we. But we're not giving up, and nor should you."

I was tired, all right. Beyond tired. If we didn't find out the status of our home soon, I thought I might run out of the house shrieking and disappear into the ponderosa pine forest, never to be seen again, except for occasional glimpses by freaked-out tourists.

I pictured the headlines: *Sasquatch sighting in the Okanagan frightens local citizens out of their wits!*

Or, better yet: *Madwoman of McDougall Creek wildfire spotted in the hills of Peachland!!*

Hmm… I mused. *She would be a good character in a fantasy novel…*

"What are you thinking about, sweetie?" Lorenzo was looking at me with worry in his eyes. "You have a strange expression."

"I'm thinking I need a change of scenery," I answered. I went over and rested my head on his shoulder, and we both sighed at the same time.

THE NEXT DAY we loaded up the car, cleaned the house, and put a 'Thank You' card and some merlot from Quail's Gate winery on the kitchen counter for our kind hosts, Peter and Paula McLaughlin. Then we left our third abode since fleeing the wildfire six days ago, and headed for the coast.

Vicky and Tony had texted us with the codes to their house and garage and many encouraging emojis to make ourselves at home. Once more, we had someone's place all to ourselves, and could mope in privacy. We were thankful for the small mercies.

It was a reprieve to be back in Tsawwassen, where I had raised my kids and worked as a fitness trainer and freelance writer for over thirty years. I had suffered tragedy and loss in this place, and it was a relief to make a fresh start in West Kelowna. But it was always awesome to reconnect with old friends here—some of whom had become so close over the years they might as well be family.

Speaking of which, only minutes after we had arrived, the doorbell rang. My long-time pal Christie stood on the step. She wore her trademark radiant smile, and brandished a bag of fresh crab she had just caught and cleaned with her dad at Boundary Bay.

"Thought you'd like some supper delivered," she chirped, putting the bag down on the counter and giving us cheerful hugs. Then, after the perfect amount of chatting, she melted away, giving us a chance to catch our breath and accustom ourselves to our new accommodations.

I went into Vicky's kitchen and organized dinner, while Lorenzo confirmed the various work meetings he had scheduled for the next day. As I tossed the salad, I wondered if I might tackle some editing before I sent my novel to my editor for the final comb-through.

Life goes on, I reflected. *Even in a catastrophe. After the first shock wave hits, and then the aftershock, you realize you still have to pull yourself together. There are other things going on...*

For instance, Lorenzo had some urgent business stuff going on tomorrow, an AGM with a tricky agenda. The evacuation had played havoc with his schedule, and now he had to make up for lost time. I also needed to play catch up with my publishing deadline.

And tomorrow morning, I'd be seeing *the Bandits* for coffee, which was bound to be a welcome distraction.

Life goes on.

Right before dinner, Lorenzo got a business call, so I took Oliver for a short walk at nearby Dennison Park. Ambling my way through the cedars and sawdust trails, I chatted with Daria, then my mom, and finally my brother in Birch Bay. Their encouraging words and outpourings of affection enveloped me like a warm blanket.

Oliver raced in circles, sniffing and wagging his tail. After all, he'd lived in Tsawwassen for ten years, from the time I got him as a six-week-old puppy, to last year when we moved to Kelowna. I knew he missed Tsawwassen, and now he revelled in all the familiar sights and smells.

Another bonus for Oliver—and us—was that there was zero smoke here, and nobody walking around with wild, panicked eyes. No wonder he was acting like a goofy little pup right now. I let him romp for an extra half an hour before we headed back. He deserved it.

As the sunlight waned, Lorenzo and I sat in the backyard, feasting on Christie's succulent crab, Caesar salad, and cheese bread. Oliver scarfed up the fallen bits and then curled on the grass with a blissful expression.

Afterward, sated and peaceful, we gazed at Vicky's garden. It was bursting with lush summer blooms: a riot of dahlias, geraniums, and begonias. However, I couldn't help but notice it seemed drier than usual for this time of year. But then, everything seemed to be changing climate-wise. I tried not to think about that—it was too overwhelming.

Lorenzo and I remained in a pensive state while dusk enclosed us, embracing this rare interlude of tranquillity. Watching afternoon transition into twilight; hearing our breathing slow, feeling our shoulders relax. Fatigued in a good way, we went back inside and turned on the evening news.

Naturally, the McDougall Creek wildfire was the top story. And because the smoke had lifted, there was lots of camera footage of the affected landscape. Fire chief Brolund had been right to warn us. The hillside looked very different. My fingernails dug into my palms and my spine went rigid as I watched.

A hideous landscape of rust-brown pine boughs and blackened trunks cut an ugly swathe under the first blue sky since the wildfire began. Any surrounding foliage beneath the giant ponderosas had simply disappeared, giving everything an eerie, fake-movie-set feel.

Fast forward: Oliver roams the wildfire-ravaged hillside

I had a sudden, vivid image of the hillside across from our house a week ago—a lifetime ago—covered with glorious crimson poppies. *Gone.* All gone.

"I'm going to bed," I said.

"I'm right behind you," Lorenzo answered in a clipped, bitter voice; switching off the remote.

Our hillside covered with poppies before the fire

LAKE SWIM NIGHTMARE

We're in Tsawwassen, getting a break from everything. I am safe from the wildfire. What a relief...

Oliver trots faithfully alongside as we walk the dyke, heading down the trail to Centennial Beach. I feed him pieces of crab from a little baggie. There's a tin bucket in my other hand, and I begin picking blackberries from the nearby bushes. After all, it is August, and blackberries are everywhere.

I cram them into my mouth, laughing. What was I worried about? There had been something, but I can't remember.

I gaze at the ocean. Beautiful Boundary Bay. Thinking how much I miss it sometimes...the sea and the sand.

Some of my best memories were swimming here with my kids when they were small, exploring tidal pools and building sandcastles. In later years, I ran along these beach trails with my marathon training clients, telling them to pace themselves and enjoy the journey.

As a puppy, Oliver learned to swim here at Centennial Beach. The bay is sheltered, and in summertime the water is warm and luxurious. We swam with lazy abandon on those August nights. Whenever Oliver got tired, he clambered onto my back, his sodden little forelegs wrapped around my shoulders, little pink tongue panting, the salty tang of his paws in my nostrils. It comforted me.

I had gotten Oliver after losing my beloved dog the year before, loneliness winning out against my better judgement. My daughter was studying medicine at UBC, and had moved in with her boyfriend, who lived close to the university. My six-week-old puppy was another Australian shepherd, but this little fur baby had one blue eye and one brown—reminding me of my kids.

Oliver loved the ocean, as did I. But we both prefer the lake. There's something about Okanagan Lake that pulls at you, heart and soul. It's so clear, and blue, and deep. Maybe it's just about me being away from tragedy. Fresh water. New surroundings...

And suddenly, in the arbitrary way of dreaming, I'm back in West Kelowna—the home that I've embraced.

We're swimming in the deep, deep lake now, not the shallow, salty bay. Oliver is on my back again, but he's heavy, because he's full grown, and I don't like the feeling. It's dark, and the water is cold. If I keep going, we might drown. What was I thinking?

I realize suddenly there's no one else around. Why are we alone?

Frantic, I strike out for the shore. But Oliver on my back is pushing me down, and I'm submerged. I flail in panic. Then, suddenly, my dog's weight is gone, floating away, dissipating in the lake. I'm liberated by the lightnesss of being unencumbered, and joy courses through me.

The fact that I am not worried about Oliver jolts me into realizing I am trapped in a dream. But a moment later the knowledge is gone.

I lift my head, gasping for air, and glimpse the shoreline. At the sight, my gasp becomes a choking scream, and I swallow a mouthful of water before regaining my breath.

The land is ablaze—all of it. Kelowna is on fire. Giant, undulating fingers of flame.

What is the point of trying to swim to shore? There is no safety to be had there. I squint, looking at a series of large humps floating along *the water, like the backs of giant tortoises, all in a line. Across the bumps, terrified figures are hopping in a panic, from one hump to the next.*

Looking closer, I see the humps are automobiles, which people have pushed into the lake. The owners are running, hopping wildly from car to truck to van to car, fleeing the fire.

The lake is the only escape from this ravenous, blazing monster. But as I gaze around me, an insidious darkness takes hold, and I know no place will ever be safe again.

This darkness is despair. I've met it before. I stop moving and let myself sink beneath the lake's surface.

There's no escaping despair.

AWAKENING FROM YET ANOTHER NIGHTMARE, I sat in bed and put my hands to my cheeks, finding them wet with tears. A bird was trilling nearby, outside the open window. I slowed my breathing, trying to dispel the illogical feeling of doom that gripped me.

The birdcall came again. It was a stellar jay—I knew the sound, one of my favourite sounds in the world. My eyes stung. I had a crazy thought: *Has Stella flown all the way down from Kelowna to Tsawwassen, just to visit me?*

It took only a moment for me to realize how absurd this was. But then, I'm a fantasy writer. *Save it for one of your novels*, I told myself sternly.

Still, I couldn't help feeling more hopeful. Maybe there were small ways to escape despair this time; and one such path might be as simple as listening to the birds sing outside my window.

19

RUNNING OUT OF UNDERWEAR

Excerpt from *Global News* Television, Wednesday August 23:
   West Kelowna's fire chief knows exactly how anxious evacuees are to get home, now that the McDougall Creek Wildfire is more manageable.
   "I appreciate all the patience you've shown," Jason Brolund said on Wednesday, speaking directly via the last Emergency Operations Centre update.
   "I'm still out of my house, as is my family. I'm feeling the same things you guys are. I'm running out of underwear too, folks."
   My reaction when I heard the fire chief utter that sentence stays with me to this day. Walking by the television, carrying two plates of sandwiches, I stared at the TV, incredulous, and then started laughing so hard the dishes almost crashed to the floor.
   It was a weird moment for Finding the Phoenix. Behind me, I heard Lorenzo's startled guffaw. "Running out of underwear!" he chortled at the TV. "I hear you, man..."
   "You're not running out," I protested, with mock-indignance. "I do laundry wherever we land." (Full disclosure: we are not a traditional couple in terms of domestic chores. For example, I do

the laundry, but he does the ironing—way, way, worse. Slave labour, in fact.)

"It's a metaphor," he explained. At the look on my face, he muttered, "I know, I know, you're the author...you're familiar with metaphors."

We both started snickering again as we watched the rest of the news conference, especially seeing Fire Chief Brolund blush after he had blurted out the underwear remark on camera.

I felt less alone. There were so many people in the *same boat* as us. Even Fire Chief Brolund. It was comforting for a moment. But I must have been wrestling with the ever-lurking PTSD spectre. Because the thought of 'boats' led to thinking of Okanagan Lake, which gave me shuddering flashbacks of my nightmare about floating in the dark water, facing a hellish orange landscape on the shoreline before me.

So, I changed the subject in my mind, telling myself to think about the future, not some stupid dream. But contemplating the unknown increased my uneasiness. I put the plates down and then bumped into Lorenzo's suitcase, stubbing my toe. I gave it a surly little kick. "Ouch!"

Lorenzo looked over, startled. "When, though?" I asked him, suddenly belligerent. "*When* do we get to find out? Underwear jokes notwithstanding. This is killing me!"

Lorenzo's expression grew serious. "We have to keep thinking about the people who already know they're going back to *nothing*." He rubbed his forehead. "Do you think *they're* happy that they 'know'? And others like Tim and Chantelle, who are also going back to a destroyed home, only packaged in a standing foundation. How do you think they feel?"

I looked at him, sick at heart for everyone who had it worse than we did. Ashamed. Seeing my face, he leaned forward and grabbed my hand, but didn't stop talking. "Our house is still there, so let's try to be thankful for that. As for the rest, we'll know when we know."

It was true. My frustration subsided. "Thanks, Jason Brolund," I murmured to the TV screen. Lorenzo gave me a minute-long hug, and then I returned to sorting the laundry, underwear and all.

THE NEXT DAY I saw a post on the West Kelowna Firefighters Facebook page, which made me laugh all over again:
"Please don't bring our chief underwear. We'll take care of him."

It turned out that a bunch of people were dropping off underwear at the fire hall. And, despite the social media comment, they continued doing so.

Finally Fire Chief Brolund addressed his enthusiastic fans during another news conference: *"I do want to say that I'm doing fine for underwear,"* he grinned. He went on to thank the public for their outpouring of support and gratitude to the firefighters (cards, posters, etc.)

Any moments of levity in this cataclysmic situation were to be clutched at like an outstretched hand when falling into an abyss. Everyone understood the underwear metaphor's purpose.

Fire Chief Brolund was pleading with us to be patient. The fire department and municipal government were taking the 'return home' process very seriously. And although evacuation orders had relaxed throughout the day, it was bound to be slow going.

He reeled off a long list of hazards in the worst-affected neighbourhoods: hoses, pumps and bladders, and other debris; scorched ground (still hot) and downed power wires; natural gas leaks and 'danger trees' (burned and ready to fall at the slightest provocation). Wounded and disoriented wildlife were wandering around.

"I'm not talking about sweeping the streets," Chief Brolund said wryly. "We're holding people back because, sometimes, we're still firefighting in your neighbourhood. I can't put you back if there's still a fire burning in your back yard—or nearby."

Brolund finished the press conference by reiterating that the Fire Department would not permit residents to go home until it was 100% safe to do so. Period.

In case you're wondering whether the authorities were being overcautious, I can attest to witnessing most of the above hazards when we finally glimpsed our neighbourhood again (before we could return home, of course).

There were also problematic matters like restoring utilities, damaged power and sewer systems, garbage collection, clean drinking water, and repairing the roads to make them safe to travel. Debris—ashes, rocks, and tree stumps that had rolled down the hillside—covered many streets.

More frightening to contemplate was the genuine possibility of conditions deteriorating. The actual fire could return. Fire Chief Brolund had made a blunt statement to that effect: "We want to avoid having to evacuate you a second time if this incident escalates."

Returning home only to receive another evacuation order would be overwhelming and traumatic. Also, according to the fire department, people are more likely to resist being evacuated the second time around.

Authorities had downgraded some of the orders, allowing more residents to return home. However, we remained under evacuation.

WE MIGHT NOT BE RUNNING out of underwear, but we were running out of patience. I became more easily irritated by trivial things: looking for spices in yet another unfamiliar kitchen; listening to Oliver whine whenever he saw us packing up our suitcases yet again. More than anything else, the oft-repeated, well-intentioned remarks made by friends and acquaintances, to the effect that 'you guys must be so overjoyed that your house didn't burn down!'

I gritted my teeth whenever someone phoned or texted congratulating us. There was nothing to rejoice about in this situation. Even if our house turned out to be utterly unscathed, were we supposed do a victory dance about having escaped incineration, when more than half of our neighbours had lost their homes?

Also, the odds of our house being intact were almost nil. The damage could be as severe as Tim and Chantelle's place, looking okay on the outside, but gutted within. Or it could be smoke and heat damaged, but not much else. Either way, we still didn't know. And we had no idea when we'd find out, so joy wasn't any part of our present equation.

We were deeply grateful, though, for the support of friends and family. And there were flickers of hope amid the smoke-clouds. Those moments when we could still joke with our neighbours (albeit dark humour), FaceTime with our kids and grandbabies, and reflect on the fact that no one had died in this fire.

It was a sobering thought. The McDougall Creek wildfire had grown so fast, and moved with such relentless savagery, it was a miracle that no lives were lost in the fallout.

Although it's obvious, I feel compelled to add that the lives at greatest risk were those of fire fighters combating the fire directly but also entering high-risk residential areas to protect and rescue residents who refused to evacuate their homes.

Following this train of thought, there is no doubt it wasn't pure luck that no one died in this fire. The West Kelowna Fire Department, led by Fire Chief Brolund, performed with astounding courage and efficiency, working in conjunction with Mayor Gord Milsom and City Council. It was awe-inspiring to hear about how courageous and tenacious our firefighters were against this ferocious monster, despite fatigue, and terrifying personal risk.

Firefighter putting out spot fires during the McDougall Creek wildfire disaster (Photo credit: BCWS via Twitter)

Even more impressive, local firefighters battled the wildfire despite the fact that many of their own homes were burning down while they fought the fire elsewhere. This was also true for some of the law enforcement officers who enforced evacuation orders and assisted the wildfire's victims, putting their own lives at risk by doing so.

The community of West Kelowna, the majority of whom pulled together in the face of this almost insurmountable catastrophe, reinforced all these factors, preventing the McDougall Creek wildfire from becoming a tragedy of even greater proportions.

I had to keep reminding myself it wasn't over yet.

After bottling up a lot emotion, I'd now get to vent when I met my group of fitness bandits for coffee.

ENTERING L'Aroma in Tsawwassen was a homecoming of sorts. The coffeeshop was a five-minute walk downhill to Centennial Beach, its meandering dike trails guarded by prehistoric looking blue herons, lush with the teeming tidepools of Boundary Bay, punctuated by driftwood and seagrass. And it was only a five minute walk the other way to Tsawwassen centre, with its quaint boutiques and restaurants. This little hamlet had remained almost unchanged for decades, and was an oasis from downtown Vancouver.

"Hi!" We 'bandits' greeted each other with unrestrained enthusiasm and were soon yakking at the trestle table we'd commandeered at the back of the cafe. Six gals were in town and able to make it, bringing with them an ocean of concern and good will. It a balm to my soul, even when someone made the remark about how overjoyed I must be to have a standing home.

When you're in crisis, being around people who've known you for many years can be the difference between overcoming an ordeal, or admitting defeat. I highly recommend the former.

With some of my Tsawwassen 'Fitness Bandits' at our favourite cofee shop, L'Aroma

By the time I had finished venting and being clucked over by a dozen fitness fiends who had transformed into mother hens, I was ready to face things again. These women saw me as *strong;*

and so I channelled my energy, dusted myself off and readied myself to return to the emotional fray.

*Full disclosure: I was at the coffee shop for three hours and had a Venti Americano and two iced lattes. I'm guessing the caffeine didn't hurt either…

20

THE DEVIL YOU KNOW

Excerpt from *Castanet* newspaper, Thursday August 24:
   STATUS OF MCDOUGALL CREEK WILDFIRE IN WEST KELOWNA REMAINS NOT HELD

Today BCWF Service confirmed that the wildfire remains "not held," so no change to yesterday's update. This means we are still in an active wildfire stage in West Kelowna. But BC Wildfire did indicate that continuing promising weather conditions since yesterday, including cooler temperatures along with 2mm of rain again last night, is providing greater stability and fire suppression.

Chef Brolund confirmed that no additional loss of structure occurred since yesterday. To date, 84 properties experienced damage or total loss. "Personal contact with property owners remains a top priority, and, for those affected, we thank you for your patience waiting for a safe return home."

On a sad note, it was revealed that Wilson's Landing Fire Department saw thirteen of their own members lose their homes in the fire.

"It was a violent end—the world shattered," described Fire Chief Paul Zydowicz when talking about the fight against the fire in Trader's Cove.

Being in the dark continued to stress me out. We didn't know how badly our home was damaged. Or when authorities would lift evacuation orders so we could return and find out. Face what had happened. Most of all, we didn't know when we could go home. If ever.

Authorities had given the green light to many neighbourhoods, meaning several thousand people could already look at their properties. When would we get our turn?

Being in limbo can make you feel powerless.

But with knowledge comes power. I decided that even if I couldn't get the answers I wanted, I could learn more about this out-of-control beast of a wildfire.

Lorenzo was in downtown Vancouver for a board meeting. Oliver and I had done a morning run along the dike, and he was snoozing contentedly on the living room rug, no doubt dreaming of the ducks he'd terrorized.

I'd been working on my almost-completed fantasy novel. However, my mind kept wandering, and finally I left the poor princess in a cave, about to be attacked by the angry-queen-of-all-monsters who had taken a disliking to her.

Real life was just as action-packed as a novel right now, and a lot more relevant. Sitting on the comfy sofa with my laptop, I began an internet search to define some phrases and terms I'd heard in the past week since the fire began.

I'd already learned about 'crowning' and 'candling' (different ways that trees ignite) so I scrolled past those, looking for other terms that were vaguely familiar.

Held, for instance. As in "the fire was still not *held*." Before becoming embroiled in the wildfire, I would have assumed it meant the fire was extinguished, or at least mostly put out.

Here's the actual definition of *being held*:

Officials believe this blaze is not likely to spread past pre-determined boundaries under specific conditions. Meaning it's nowhere near "extinguished." Just contained. For now. Unless conditions change. Which could happen.

Of note is another term, even more cryptic. As in "this

remains a wildfire *of note."* Definition: The fire continues to be highly visible and/or presents a threat to public safety.

All this was good to know. Or was it?

Oliver began whining to go outside, so I zipped through the rest of my self-imposed tutorial: ranking wildfire behavior.

Rank 1 is the least threatening (a smouldering ground fire, with no open flame. From there it goes all the way to Rank 6 (a blow-up, or conflagration, extremely aggressive fire behavior).

I'd read that the McDougall Creek fire was a Rank 5, which made me so queasy I had to close my eyes for a few seconds and take some deep breaths before I could keep reading. This inferno was almost the worst a fire could be without being an actual major explosion. The elemental fear, that of prey-fleeing-predator, no longer seemed a figment of my overwrought imagination. It seemed like reality.

LATER IN THE afternoon of August 24, a cheerful newscaster with a booming voice announced that all evacuation orders for the City of Kelowna were lifted, and residents could begin returning to their properties. West Kelowna was another matter, however. Authorities had lifted orders for a very few properties, but we were not on the list.

Unaware of the distinction between the two communities (and/or missing the part that said *"some people"*), well-meaning acquaintances reached out to applaud us on our return home. I tried to rein in my annoyance, which was just despondence on steroids at this point.

I wasn't alone. Chantelle texted me to vent about people enthusing about how their house was still standing, when in fact it was a gutted facade. I replied in kind.

One of the worst things about this is that people keep texting, phoning, or emailing me with the supposedly joyful news that we are allowed to go home, not getting that WE ARE

FINDING THE PHOENIX

NOT ALLOWED TO GO HOME. I want to scream at them, "Please don't send me these messages based on vague news updates talking about our general area! You don't know what the F you are talking about. If I could go home, don't you think I'd be the first to know?" But I can't say that, it would be mean, because they are so well-intentioned.

Looking back now, I cringe at how grumpy I was; but then I remind myself that people under severe stress/trauma get irritated more easily. The best tip in responding to people who are putting their foot in their mouth and making you feel worse? Stay cordial but cut the conversation short if you need to. And remind yourself they are reaching out because they are thinking of you and wishing you well.

WE WERE STILL at Vicky and Tony's in Tsawwassen on Friday, August 26, when Prime Minister Justin Trudeau arrived in the Okanagan to meet with leaders. He convened with Chief Robert Louie of the Westbank First Nation (WFN), Mayor Milsom, Fire Chief Brolund, and others at the the WFN government offices.

At a news conference for national media, Trudeau did his best to reassure rattled nerves. I listened to his speech on the CBC that evening.

Chief Louie with Prime Minister Trudeau at WFN offices

PM Trudeau in Kelowna reviewing map of McDougall Creek wildfire (Photo credit: La Presse Canadienne/Marissa Tiel)

"We will be there to make sure we're not just learning the lessons we're taking through these very difficult moments, but that we are applying the lessons, and that we are increasing our resources and our ability to keep people safe going forward," he said.

I hoped this was true. That next time around our local firefighters had access to more resources, and the ESS would also have more support in place to help evacuees.

I realized I had a bigger hope: there wouldn't be a next time.

But the fire hadn't finished with us yet. It still raged out of control as the weekend came and went. Evacuation orders had been lifted in other affected area communities like Lake Country, but a large number of people in West Kelowna remained displaced. BCWS and city officials reminded us that even when the fire was finally under control and we were all able to return to our neighbourhoods, it would be weeks, if not months, before some people's lives returned to normal.

We were going back to the West Kelowna area on Tuesday. What had happened since we left? Revelations of staggering devastation in our community, from a wildfire that still wouldn't quit. But the most important thing for us was confirming our house was standing, which was a momentous piece of news and an enormous relief, although there was no word yet about whether it was habitable.

The McDougall Creek wildfire evacuation had lasted almost two weeks, and there was no end in sight. I went to bed and dreamed I was home...

∼

SPRINKLER NIGHTMARE

In my dream, we are back home on Bear Creek Road, and I have just stepped out the front door of our house. In a kind of trance, I begin to wander around our burned neighbourhood. Crossing the street to where the trailhead starts, I amble along the grass, stopping to gaze down the steep hillside. Rows of burned trees stand before me, like rust-coloured sentinels. The grass is crispy beneath my sneakers.

As I continue down the trail, the patches of dry, rustling grass become sparse, replaced by grey, dusty, soil, which I realize is actually ash. Sadly I squat down, grazing the ash with my fingertips.

All at once I notice a length of slender black rubber hose weaving among the withered stalks of grass and gnarled tree roots. This is baffling.

Is it irrigation? It can't be a firefighting hose, that's so much thicker. Plus, one of a firefighter's main prerogatives is to never leave hose behind. As I ponder, a sprinkler suddenly turns on, its hissing noise making me jump. It must be a water hose!

But how could it turn on by itself?

The water spurts out onto the parched ground, and I am grateful to see the moisture darkening the earth. This summer has been so dry, that's what caused the...

Something strange is happening. Aghast, I watch as the dark patches of ground start glowing, and then little smouldering flames crop up. There is a ravenous crackling sound as the fire sparks along the ashy ground.

Everything is burning, even though there is nothing left to burn.

Water from the sprinklers created this fire. How ironic, how hideous. Desperate, frantic, struggling to breathe, I run along the length of the hose. I need to see where it starts, so I can stop the fire.

I scream, "Turn it off!" Looking around for someone—anyone—to help me stop this.

But no one is there, and my shout echoes down the gully as flames engulf the landscape.

21

PARADISE LOST

Excerpt from *Global News* TV, Tuesday August 29, 2023
As progress continues to be made on parts of the McDougall Creek wildfire burning in the hills above West Kelowna, residents in one of the hardest hit neighbourhoods get the green light to finally return home.

While some of the residents were fortunate enough to see their homes still standing, others weren't. Multiple homes throughout the area sustained either partial or significant damage. And for other homeowners, they'll be returning to nothing...

Global News tried speaking with several residents who came back to nothing but ashes and rubble, but they were understandably emotional and declined...

Duh.

On Tuesday morning I stood in Vicky's back yard, breathing in the early morning air, noticing a slight chill as summer neared its end. Oliver panted lightly beside me on the vibrant green lawn, keeping a vigilant eye out for squirrels and crows.

Lorenzo was inside, brewing coffee and energetically moving bags toward the front entrance. After almost two weeks of sheltering elsewhere, we were finally going back to West Kelowna. But what were we driving toward? Why had this happened to us?

Remnants of my firehose nightmare clung to me like little rubber tentacles.

I walked around the backyard, gazing at Vicky's lush flowerbeds, silently asking the universe for answers. The dahlias nodded sagely toward me in the summer breeze but offered no other wisdom. I heard my husband's voice calling me and turned to go inside.

Wandering into the kitchen, I beheld Lorenzo beaming at me across Vicky's kitchen island, a cup of coffee beside him and his computer in front of him. He lifted the laptop aloft like he was brandishing a winning lottery ticket, and did a little jig.

"What is it?" I asked, wary. Had he finally cracked? "What's all the excitement about?"

"I'm on the CORD website," he told me. "The verdict just came in on our house..." He paused dramatically. "No major structural damage!" He put his laptop down and started two-stepping again, eyes shining.

No major structural damage. I gaped at him in silence for about ten seconds, and then gave a demented screech. We clasped hands across the counter.

"But what about the inside?" Bizarre images flashed through my mind of partially collapsed rooms, beams lying across couches, piles of bricks, broken glass.

"We don't know yet. But it means that at least everything is still intact with the foundation," Lorenzo watched me wrestle with my emotions. "That's a good thing, right?"

I nodded in agreement, letting relief flood me. Refusing to give in to the anxiety.

"Right."

Lorenzo came to stand beside me in Vicky's kitchen, hugging me tight, while Oliver nestled up to us, sharing in the moment. We were among the lucky ones.

∼

FINDING THE PHOENIX

Driving along the Coquihalla Highway just past Hope, our surroundings looked serene. The treeline had not yet changed from lush evergreen Fraser Valley forest to the sparser landscape of the Interior. Blue sky, light traffic. What more could you ask for?

But my stomach had been clenched since this morning, and Lorenzo was tapping the steering wheel in a rapid staccato rhythm, fuelling my unpleasant jolts of adrenaline. *Join a band*, I silently urged him. *Become a mid-life drummer. Get it out of your system...*

Of course what bothered us was that we couldn't get into our neighbourhood yet—it was still too dangerous. But it was killing us to be going *back* without going *home*.

We were lucky beyond measure to be able to stay at Jay and Jeanette's place, though, and we knew it. Their house is just off Boucherie Road on the 'Winery Trail'—also in West Kelowna, but on the other side of Highway 97, so therefore unscathed by the McDougall Creek wildfire.

(Sidebar: Weeks later, Fire Chief Jason Brolund would reveal that the last line of hope for controlling the wildfire was the highway itself. Scary.)

~

It was the last leg of our journey back to West Kelowna. Merritt had good gas prices, so we stopped to fuel up. Lorenzo was in the gas station store buying a Snickers bar, which I hoped might distract him from his drumming. I paced outside to stretch my cramped legs, reading a text from Chantelle.

We don't even know when we can get there to assess the damage. And we don't know how to deal with our horrible ambivalence about dealing with what's left of our neighbourhood and homes. Want to see vs dread it...

I had the same ambivalence, along with a growing sense of guilt that our house was still standing.

We'd entered a different realm—now dealing with solid decisions and practicalities that Chantelle and Tim and the other 'total loss' neighbours were not. This scenario had both positive and negative elements, the positive being, of course, that we didn't have to start from scratch. But there were obstacles to tackle which we never could have imagined.

For example, the fridge/freezer debacle.

While I was reading Chantelle's text, I got an email alert in my inbox from our efficient Royal Heights Properties strata president, Judith Harris. This was something never to ignore, as all specific information about our neighbourhood came funneled through Judith Harris (in your head, just call her 'the other Judith').

I closed Chantelle's text and opened the email message, scanning it with a racing pulse. The subject line:

"ATTACHED: LOCAL AUTHORITIES HAVE SENT THE STRATA COUNCIL FURTHER UPDATES ON OUR NEIGHBOURHOOD."

The BC Wildfire Service attachment began by reminding us that the houses on our street that were still standing—potentially livable—would *all* have smoke and heat damage because of the sustained intensity of the wildfire.

But there was another problem that hadn't even occurred to us: any fridges or freezers with food inside them (meaning all of them) would have to be replaced, because the food was by now so rotten it would have morphed into biohazardous waste, destroying the appliances, the floors, and making the household environment dangerous.

I got a dark moment of amusement about it, envisioning the old horror movie "The Blob". But the rest of the email wiped the grin off my face. BCSW warned us to be aware of "toxic ooze" and "poisonous vapours." When entering our homes, under no circumstances should we open our fridges/freezers. Instead, we should stay away or duct tape the doors—with gloved hands—if they had gaped open.

Good grief.

Restoration company technicians trained in disposing of biohazardous waste would be called to remove the appliances, and they'd be wearing hazmat suits. All property owners should wear masks inside their homes, because of the likelihood of noxious odours emanating from the waste, as well as carcinogenic residual particles from the wildfire smoke.

Marvellous. Any fantasies I was harbouring about an idyllic homecoming were punctured. This was becoming even more surreal than our evacuation.

As I read on, the warnings grew more forbidding. If we were foolish enough to handle or open our fridges/freezers, our home insurance would become void. *What??*

In closing, authorities recommended we hurry up and order new appliances, because there would be a "run on them" in the next few weeks. There were hundreds of other people in our situation.

We had a fridge/freezer upstairs in the kitchen, a bar fridge/freezer on the deck, and a stand-up freezer in the garage. In the tenant's suite, we also had a fridge/freezer.

"We'd better stop at Rona on the way through and do some fridge shopping," Lorenzo said, ever-practical.

I shook my head. "I'm not in the mood."

"Up to you." Lorenzo raised an eyebrow. "But do you want to be without a fridge when we go back home?"

"Who knows when we're even going to be allowed to *look* at our place?" I was not to be deterred from my brooding. "The email didn't even mention a date. *When it's safe to do so,* they keep saying." I heard my voice sounding like a sullen four-year-old, and winced.

"What about Mahadev?" Lorenzo's pointed question reminded me that we needed to prepare the suite for our tenant's return to school. Mahadev was waiting anxiously at his parents' home in Calgary for the go-ahead to come back and begin his second year at UBC. The university remained closed because of the wildfire state of emergency, but everyone was hoping it would reopen in time for the start of school.

"Okay," I sighed, jolted back into being a responsible adult. "Rona, it is…"

∼

LATER THAT AFTERNOON I began coughing after we'd been to Rona and taken Oliver for a brief walk. "It's probably just allergies," I told Lorenzo, as we got back in the car.

He shrugged. "Maybe we should check the air quality. Don't forget we're back in the danger zone."

And so we were. Pulling up the weather app on my phone, I saw that the air quality was "9," which was almost as bad as it could get without having to stay indoors and seal up the window cracks.

Again, I marvelled at how the toxicity level could be so high in the absence of any detectable smell—no smoke, no burning, no chemical odors. Looking around, there was nothing dramatic to see either in terms of smoke or fog, just the perpetual, eerie twilight; the sun transformed into a weird red-ringed disk behind a dreary grey sky.

The lack of colour and light suddenly seemed like the most dreary thing I had ever contemplated.

"At least we have shiny new fridges," I said. Staring at the windshield, unable to keep the sarcasm from my voice. "Once we plug them in, why don't we climb inside the freezers and cryogenically suspend ourselves until all this is over?"

"You're a fantasy writer," Lorenzo reminded me, without missing a beat. He turned on the ignition and adjusted the rearview mirror. "You haven't written sci-fi in years. Stay in your lane." (Can you see why I love my husband?)

On that note, we headed toward Boucherie Road, where our next accommodations awaited.

As we drove along Boucherie's winery trail, with its rows of ripening grape vines enticing visitors and locals alike, we were the exceptions, barely glancing at the burgeoning fruit.

Lorenzo turned on the car radio for news updates, and I looked down at my phone. Another text alert had just come in from Chantelle. I glanced at it.

Welcome home, girl!

"What are you smiling about?" Lorenzo asked. "I thought you were all grumpy about being at Rona for so long."

Truth be told, being called 'girl' had given me a little glow, if only briefly. At my age, you take what you can get... Also, it sounded like Chantelle was excited to see me.

We had forged such good friendships up here in the Okanagan, and the wildfire monster couldn't take that away, no matter what else it had destroyed. I put my hand on Lorenzo's knee and gave it a squeeze. "I'm happy to be back."

And despite everything, I was.

22

STANDING IN THE QUEUE

Excerpt from *Castanet* **Newspaper**, June 2024 (this year):

Significant changes are coming to the Emergency Support Services program in the Central Okanagan. The volunteer organization that cares for evacuees in emergency situations came under fire during last year's McDougall Creek Wildfire, when as many as 24,000 Westside residents were forced from their homes in a 72-hour period.

"What happened last year was unprecedented," said Jason Bedell, who has been hired to manage the ESS program going forward. "It's my strongly held belief that ESS was not set up to handle any event like last year. It was beyond our capacity."

Exhausted wildfire evacuees waiting at ESS centre (Photo credit: Madison Reeve/File

As already mentioned, we didn't have occasion to visit our ESS support centre more than a few times. But many McDougall Creek wildfire evacuees depended on it. So, I'd like to take a moment to recall some of the things, good and bad, about what our government offered to those people in need at a dire time.

Those thousands of us forced to flee our homes with less than 24 hours' notice.

I confess guilt grips me whenever I get dramatic about this evacuation, coming as I do from a democratic country with free health care and a robust social services support system. A country of safety and plenty, compared with many other places. So, I feel guilty when I say "flee." Complaining sometimes seems self-indulgent.

That being said, I've experienced tragedy of the worst kind. Because of this, I can instantly identify trauma.

Trauma includes, of course, the psychological effects of a sudden disruption or loss of health, home, stability, or the death of someone you love.

I bring this up to emphasize how upsetting it was for traumatized evacuees who didn't get adequate support when they needed it most. Although the ESS was doing what it could, there was a veritable flood of applicants, desperate and afraid. Many with kids and pets, who were hungry, and tired, and disoriented. It was a gong show.

The lineups were long and excruciating. The systems were slow in processing evacuees' inputted data. Information was sometimes confusing and contradictory.

But we can't blame the volunteers themselves for any of that, because they were volunteering out of good-heartedness and a genuine desire to help. And they were often also fatigued, harassed, and afraid. Fear and dread are contagious.

Because of this, some of them were abrupt or not as patient as they could have been. But most ESS volunteers were *wonderful!*

We were more fortunate than some evacuees, who waited days for support, even if it was just to get into a hotel for shelter.

Premier David Eby, when visiting, declared that it was unacceptable, the provincial government called in staff from service BC to help—900 people to support the overworked ESS volunteers.

Jules, one of the wonderful ESS volunteers

Jules was one of those wonderful people. When we first went to the ESS shelter, it was after we were back in West Kelowna. We were trying to get remuneration for those friends who sheltered us during the evacuation, as well as vouchers for our food/clothing expenses (we were eating out mostly, and of course almost all our clothes were at home).

After a tense exchange with a receptionist who questioned our identification, making me pull out multiple cards and scrutinizing them so methodically it became torturous; and another stressful moment when I found out they were escorting Oliver to a "dog zone" instead of allowing him to accompany us to our application interview, I was assigned to a specific table, and finally landed up with Jules.

Thank God for Jules.

I was battling waves of irritation and anxiety. In retrospect, I have a teensy feeling I overreacted with the receptionist, or as they called her 'the greeter.'

(Later, as we were departing after my meeting with Jules, she handed me a card with the contact number for free crisis counselling, which I accepted, being in a better frame of mind by then).

Anyway. Irritation. Anxiety. Nettled by my little spat with the greeter, I was downright grumpy by the time I got to the table where they'd sent me. The centre was situated in a cavernous room. In normal times, it functioned as the gymnasium in the

Mount Boucherie Secondary School. Now it was a makeshift Emergency Support Services centre; lit with cold fluorescent lights and crammed with rows of identical tables and chairs. ESS staff occupied one side of the table and evacuees the other. It was reminiscent of an ICBC office where you went to grudgingly pay a speeding ticket fine (more Lorenzo's territory than mine, haha.)

I finally found my assigned table #23, presided over by an elderly man who stood politely as I approached. "Well hello there, young lady!"

Jules was a spectacled, white-haired gent with a lined, weathered face and a warm smile. Still disgruntled, I didn't smile back. I regarded him suspiciously, and glanced repeatedly through the glass pane of the closed door at Lorenzo, who had promised to keep an eye on Oliver in the cordoned-off dog section. Several big dogs were there, and Oliver was easily intimidated because of a coyote attack when he was less than a year old.

Lorenzo kept his other eye on me, doubtless because I was acting even more skittish than my dog. He was obviously trying to be supportive, and kept grinning and waving at me through the glass. From where I stood, he succeeded only in looking completely deranged. I shook my head in annoyance. It was like a horde of buzzing flies had settled on my shoulders.

"Ahem..." Jules sat again, shuffling some papers and drumming his fingers on the tabletop. His tone was jovial though, not impatient. "Have a seat."

I slumped down in the chair opposite him, my adrenaline dissipating and numbness creeping in. Mumbling,"I'm tired of all this."

He nodded with a sympathetic grimace. "Boy, oh boy, I bet you must be! This is just plain 'crazy town', if you know what I mean. The McDougall Creek wildfire is the scariest thing I've ever witnessed in these parts. And I've been here for longer than you can imagine."

Leaning forward and lowering his voice confidentially, Jules added, "I must confess it's hard to keep track of what we're doing at the moment in these centres. There's too many evacuees —it's pandemonium. But I'll help sort you out as best I can."

His voice was so kind. Tears slid down my cheeks, and Jules handed me a tissue. "Everything's going to be okay," he said. "This is a great community. We'll get through this together." He paused with a smile, then took something out of his pocket and pushed it across the table. It was a dog biscuit.

"Can't forget about the little fella," Jules said, winking. I smiled back at him through my tears.

Besides Jules, there was the lovely ESS pet support woman who tried to rescue Nash's goldfish, and then stood in front of Chantelle and Tim's home, crying helplessly for our burned neighbourhood. I don't know her name, but if I saw her I'd hug her.

The ESS volunteers are a wonderful crew, and we were lucky to have them. Although the system isn't perfect, its support workers forma part of the community bedrock that helps bolster victims in the midst of a catastrophe, giving them a booster shot of hope to get through a deeply frightening time in their lives.

23

THE MAGIC SCHOOL BUS

Excerpt from the City of West Kelowna, Wednesday August 30, 2023

    Today, West Kelowna Fire Chief Jason Brolund provided the update below.

"Yesterday, August 29th, the McDougall Creek wildfire threatened our community in a new way," says West Kelowna fire chief Jason Brolund. "The transition from warm stable weather to cooler, wet days brought increased winds. By mid-morning yesterday, we learned that the transition could be more violent and accompanied by strong winds and low humidity. These factors are a recipe for increased fire behavior...

"We were not going to take any risks, and took decisive action to protect the community...The Evacuation Alert was expanded to keep the public alert and prepared...Yesterday 28 fire apparatus and close to 125 firefighters were engaged on the ground in Glenrosa and Smith Creek alone...

"Today, we are feeling better about the weather forecast and fire conditions in West Kelowna. However, this wildfire will be an ongoing threat for a while to come...The rain last night and in the coming days will help, but it will not put the fire out.

"I urge the public to remain vigilant and alert today and, in the *days ahead, we will continue to focus on the safe return of evacuees to the most damaged neighbourhoods of West Kelowna..."*

Luckily, it was not until that evening when I read the mixed-message update. Instead of indulging in my usual angsting, I had put my worries aside, and we spent a pleasant, non-smoky (for once) afternoon lounging in the pool at our friends' Jay and Jeanette's place.

During some rare time off, Daria and Sean had brought baby Maya over, and Sean dunked her in the pool while Daria petted Oliver and smiled at their antics, and I whipped up shrimp tacos in the kitchen.

Even in two weeks Maya had grown, and at almost six months was crawling on all fours. Her blue eyes and one-toothed grin lit up my world.

It was a much-needed reprieve from the stress. The skies were smoke free, and we could pretend everything was normal. Almost.

Going back inside, I saw an email from strata president Judith Harris. Authorities had arranged a bus tour for Royal Heights residents to go through the neighbourhood and view their properties. The catch was that only those with totally destroyed homes had received invitations. And no one could get off the bus at any point.

Wow.

Right as I read the email, Chantelle began texting me, and I tried to respond and flip tacos at the same time.

She didn't mince words. **WTF???????**

I typed back, my fingers flying on the keyboard. *No kidding! Are you going on the bus? Seems like it would be frustrating that you can't get off, even just to look around the outside of your house and yard. But I guess it's too dangerous.*

As I waited for Chantelle's response, I tried not to think about how this dubious excursion might divide our neighbourhood. Some could go on the tour, some could not. Not a good formula for feel-good vibes.

And the fact that WE can't go on the bus, I couldn't help adding. *Almost like being penalized for not having a full structural loss.*

I'm sure I could get you on as my plus one, she shot back. **Tim's not interested in going.**

Rule breaker, I thought with fondness. *Just like me. It's more of a young person's game, though.*

I wouldn't go if you paid me, I texted.

Okay, I'm not going either.

With your sleuthing skills, we can probably find out more about the neighbourhood than being on a 'Magic School Bus for Depressives' tour.

Haha. I could almost hear her mirthless laughter. **You're cracking me up.**

I put down my phone to plate up our patio lunch, and as we gathered around the table. "Guess what I just found out?" I said, and told them about the tour.

"Why do you keep calling it 'the Magic School Bus tour'?" Daria asked as I handed around the tacos. She raised her voice to be heard above Maya's shrieks of delight when Oliver settled himself beneath her high chair (dogs know where the best scraps are).

"Oh, I was being facetious." I put the tray down beside Daria, and Oliver eyed it with disappointment. He's not a shrimp fan. "The bus tours are only for the worst hit neighbourhoods, and only for people whose place is a total loss. So I named it 'the Magic School Bus Tour for Depressives'."

Daria pulled a wry face. "So basically everyone on that bus is going to be bawling their eyes out the whole time."

"Pretty much."

"That doesn't seem like the best idea."

"Nope." I shrugged. But there isn't much of a road map to work with."

"There are wildfires in the Okanagan all the time."

"Not like this one."

All at once the summer sun shining down on me seemed unbearably hot. I put my plate down and slipped into the cooling water of the pool.

~

THAT NIGHT the texts between us Royal Heights neighbours were flying back and forth at lightning speed. Colleen and Pierre seemed both intrigued and appalled by the concept of a bus tour. But their house was standing, so they weren't on the list. Anyway, they were still in Edmonton.

Pierre says it would have been fun to just leap out of the bus and run into our houses, Colleen joked. **What are they going to do, arrest us? I told him he's been watching too many action movies lately.**

Raj was worried because they hadn't invited her on the bus tour, and I had to keep reminding her this was a *good thing*, because it meant their home wasn't a total loss. I worried she was in the throes of another anxiety attack, because she kept obsessing about what her parents would say when she couldn't give them a firsthand update. I tried to calm her down.

I'm thinking this situation won't last long, Raj. Chantelle's been following community chats of other neighbourhoods, and the pattern seems to be that residents are allowed back to see their homes a day or two after the tour. So our street is probably almost ready. Hang tight.

Okay, Judith. I will.

I hoped we were right. Now that seeing our homes seemed imminent, the suspense was almost intolerable.

But there was no way I wanted to be on the Magic School Bus. It would be the worst of all worlds, seeing the general devastation, being unable to exit the bus to investigate the state of your own property.

The time on the stove clock said 5:27. The bus tour was about to depart for the Royal Heights community. I'd busied myself with dinner preparations, trying to stay keep myself distracted and stop second-guessing myself. (*Should I have gone with Chantelle as her 'plus one' instead of talking her out of going?*)

As if we had a psychic connection, my phone buzzed with a text notification from Chantelle.

I talked to Dan at the strata meeting last night, and he says a lot of the people in our development aren't going. We've all seen enough with the aerial footage and binoculars from the top of the highway.

I felt affirmed. *Ya, I'd rather wait longer and see the damage standing on my own two feet, not crammed into a jungle safari.*

Haha. Jungle safari. Lots of howls and shrieks as the devastation tour rolls through the neighbourhood. You're killing me.

I'd rather whimper in relative privacy...

"Are you two still yukking it up with your black humour?" Lorenzo asked, walking by and catching me giggling into my phone.

"Laugh so you don't cry," I retorted, trying to gather my dignity.

THE NEXT MORNING was smoky again, and I caught an actual whiff of burning this time. It was almost certainly Glenrosa, the suburb of Westbank closest to the highway heading west, toward Vancouver. That's where the firefighters were focusing right now. I was glad we had decided to spend yesterday sitting by the pool and visiting with family, because there wouldn't be any lounging outside today.

My phone buzzed with a text from Chantelle, who continued to amaze me with her up-to-the-minute cache of information. Apparently, there had been an unexpected twist on the Magic School Bus tour. Fire Chief Jason Brolund and Mayor Gord Milsom had both been on the bus.

No way!?

Way...

The Magic School Bus Devastation Tour

I felt a stab of profound regret that I hadn't gone with Chantelle on the tour. Like everyone else in West Kelowna, by this time I had a serious platonic crush on our fire chief. And I'd never met our highly-respected mayor, Gordon Milsom, who was also getting accolades on how he'd handled the crisis.

I tried to think of a witty rejoinder and failed. *That was nice of them.*

Yes, it was. But otherwise the bus tour went pretty much as we expected.

Meaning?

People cried, vented, hyperventilated, yelled, and the quieter ones buried their faces in their neighbours' laps.

You're making that last thing up.

I'm hanging out with a fiction writer, and I think it's influencing me. LOL.

I sent her an eye roll emoji. 😳

Did anyone say anything about our houses? I hesitated, thinking it was selfish to ask this.

Not much that we didn't already know. Like the fact that

my front door is smashed in and broken glass everywhere. Our firefighter friend Scott already told us that's how they put the fire out. Otherwise, your place would've been burned down. Remember?**

I remembered. Chantelle had mentioned before that their firefighter friend had told them there was damage on the roof from water-bombing and that the firefighters had broken into their house with axes in order to put out the blaze.

But I hadn't truly made the connection until now that our place would not be standing if they hadn't done that. My mind reeled.

Anyway, she continued. **Now we'll see if the prediction comes true. We'll see if we're allowed back in our neighbourhood in the next couple of days.**

Fingers crossed. 🤞

But I secretly doubted we'd ever be allowed back home. My pessimism was increasing with every hour went by, and it was almost easier to expect the worst than hope for good news.

I went to bed that night praying for a peaceful night's sleep. I was getting tired of the nightmares.

24

AN END TO THE WAIT

Excerpt from *CBC* News, August 31, 2023
B.C. EXTENDING STATE OF EMERGENCY DUE TO WILDFIRES AS WINDS EXPECTED TO FAN FLAMES IN NORTHEAST.

Gusts up to 60 km/h amid heat and drought expected to increase fire activity, forecaster says.

Emergency Management Minister Bowinn Ma says B.C. is extending a state of emergency due to the ongoing wildfires that have devastated parts of the province. Ma announced the two-week extension at a provincial update on drought and wildfires on Thursday.

The state of emergency, which was initially declared on Aug. 18, gives the province extended powers to respond to disasters such as wildfires.

Excerpt from *Nanaimo News* Bulletin, August 31, 2023

The McDougall Creek wildfire remains out of control in West Kelowna.

Residents of Lake Country and Kelowna might be able to rest easy after the Central Okanagan Emergency Centre announced today that the wildfires burning close to their homes are now considered under control…

Exactly two weeks after the McDougall Creek wildfire spread across Okanagan Lake, the BC Wildfire Service announced that the Clarke Creek and Walroy Lake fires are being held and under control. However, across the lake near West Kelowna, the McDougall Creek wildfire is an estimated 13, 712 hectares in size (almost 34,000 acres) and continues to burn out of control...

It was a hot Thursday afternoon in Westbank. Walking Oliver along the lakeside path at Gellatly Park, I saw the plume of smoke over to the right, north of me. *Glenrosa.*

The McDougall Creek wildfire had been burning out of control for two weeks. We had been out of our home ever since. Would this never end? The sickening notion persisted that the wildfire was a diabolical fiend, out to get *me*. No amount of rational thinking could banish my dread. I imagined it skulking and smouldering in a parallel path through the trails in Glenrosa, stalking me as I walked westward.

It was getting hotter. Oliver stopped following me and sat, panting while he made his decision; then waded into the lake to cool off. I had the irrational urge to jump into the water with him, fully clothed.

My cell phone rang. It was my mother. "Are you using the cushion?" she asked.

I had seen her briefly when we were in Tsawwassen, and she'd given me a little cushion to hold in case I got stressed out. I told her yes, and sent her a pic Lorenzo had taken of me snuggling the pillow in an emotional moment (it's a Christmas pillow, haha).

Mom had been watching the news from her home in Birch Bay, Washington (she'd married an American decades ago and became a dual citizen). The conflicting messages confused her. She'd read somewhere that Kelowna wildfire evacuees were returning home. Then another newscast reported the fire was raging on, defying suppression efforts. She wanted to know if the fire was out or not? Could Lorenzo and I go home?

Taking comfort from my mom's cushion in a dark moment

I told her it wasn't out, but it wasn't active in our neighbourhood anymore. But as she exclaimed in relief, I emphasized that we couldn't even enter our neighbourhood yet, let alone go home. There were still too many hazards.

"Don't worry, Mom," I told her. "I'll let you know when we can go back. Because that's going to be a huge day for us. Big news!" I tried not to sound testy, but it was hard.

Because the obstacles were formidable.

Some details not reported on the provincial and national news outlets were available on the Central Okanagan Emergency Operations website (CORD) and we'd seen them yesterday. The wildfire had caused significant damage to the electrical infrastructure in the area:

Approximately 27 kilometres of power lines, 359 poles, and 66 other pieces of equipment needed to be replaced. And besides the downed power lines, damaged trees, other debris, exposed gas lines, unstable terrain (gaping holes, slippery patches of soot and ash) and 'hot spots' from the blaze, were all lurking in our neighbourhood, posing risks to anyone who ventured in unaware.

No wonder we couldn't go home.

Downed power poles being replaced (Photo credit: B.C. Hydro)

I opened my mouth to tell my mom some of the stats, but she was ahead of me with her own numbers, asking me whether I knew that there were over 400 active wildfires currently burning in British Columbia. They had categorized more than 188 as out-of-control, she added.

Mom sounded horrified, but

also fascinated. I knew this was because she prided herself on keeping up with current events; but I still couldn't help replying tersely that there was only *one* wildfire I was concerning myself with right now—the one that had forced us from our home.

The phone chat ended with endearments, but on a slightly awkward note. Replaying it in my mind as I skipped stones into the lake, I squirmed. *Why had I been so on edge talking with my mother?*

Maybe because it was September 1st, and irrational though it was, I had thought that once September began, summer was basically over, and the summer wildfire nightmare would have ended.

SCHOOL WAS STARTING AGAIN SOON. The University of British Columbia (UBC) had announced they were about to open their doors—a week late—and our tenant Mahadev was now searching for a temporary place to stay once he returned from Calgary. Just in case.

"Don't worry about me, you guys," he said, "just take care of yourselves. I'll be fine for the next while, I just have to find an in between place."

But we soon realized this was not going to be easy. So many other evacuated students were also scrambling for accommodation. Kelowna was going to be a chaotic place for the next while, that was the new reality.

Autumn had crept in. The weather was cooling down, except for the odd spike in temperature—like today. Back-to-school shoppers thronged the malls. I knew this because we had gone to Sport Chek yesterday to take advantage of the 40% discount they were giving evacuees. In a kind of frenzy, I bought a bunch of replacement fitness clothes and a step. I was determined to resume teaching my online Zoom fitness classes, regardless of where I was living.

I had a sudden, absurd image of myself leading a Zumba class in the middle of a downtown intersection; and started laughing out loud, then stopped abruptly. Was I going crazy?

It was almost fall, and we were still evacuated. Enough already.

ON SATURDAY, September 2nd, Oliver and I returned home from hiking at Mt. Boucherie. The haze had eclipsed any picturesque vistas from the top, and I was unusually short of breath by the end. Checking the air quality on my phone's weather app and finding it read "10," I realized I should have stayed inside. But there's such a thing as mental health, and I refused to berate myself.

As I pulled into the driveway, I saw Lorenzo getting out of his vehicle, laden with Canadian Tire bags. He had inspected Jay and Jeanette's house for any minor repairs that needed doing to express our appreciation for letting us stay there. It also helped keep him busy. He was missing the yard maintenance and home projects that usually occupied him at our place.

I offered to make sandwiches before we continued our day. As I was slicing tomatoes, the phone rang. It was Daria.

"Mom—I just looked at the CORD website. The evacuation order for Royal Heights has been lifted!!"

"What???" I almost stabbed my hand with the paring knife.

It had finally happened. We could go see our home.

Lorenzo and I didn't know whether to laugh or cry. We usually checked the CORD website every hour or two, sometimes more—it had become a compulsion at this point—but we hadn't done so today, because it was a long weekend, and besides, they never posted anything before 10:00 a.m.

Shocked, we wandered around restlessly for a few moments, bumping into things like we were blind. Then, in silent accord, we bolted for the car.

FINDING THE PHOENIX

We left Oliver to fend for himself at Jay and Jeanette's place, much to his displeasure. But we didn't know what we'd find, and our dog was better off away from us and our escalating stress levels.

Driving up Bear Creek Road's hairpin curve, Lorenzo and I held hands, bracing ourselves for the sight of our neighbourhood, knowing it might be awful to see.

And it was.

THE FIRST THING we saw was that the vinyl fence around our gated community had melted, giving the scene a bizarre quality, almost as if it was a movie set.

Burned trees, most of them massive ponderosa pines, stood in silent stands, rusty orange needles and charred trunks, or else lay strewn and toppled about the surrounding hillside.

Melted fence and broken gate at our RHP entrance

There was "DO NOT ENTER" caution tape, plus signs that read "DANGER: WILDFIRE ZONE." I got out of the car and took down the yellow tape so we could drive through. But everywhere we looked, we saw those warnings. Somehow feeling like I was doing something risky, even criminal.

Our neighbourhood had become a danger zone

The day had dawned like many in the past couple of weeks, monochromatic and dreary. Our burned-out neighbourhood scene only increased the dystopian vibes. Worst of all were the ruined piles of rubble—metal, stone, timber and glass—all that remained of so many of our neighbours' homes.

There was no one else in sight.

We inched the vehicle up to #7, third house from the top of the hill on the left. My thighs were shaking and I put my hands on them to make them stop. Lorenzo's face was set in stone as we turned into our driveway.

At first sight, our home looked so intact it was eerie. Twin pots of geraniums still flanked the garage and were still blooming. But flames from the wildfire had burned right up to our front door, as was evidenced by blackened shrubs and trees in our front yard, and embers scattered across the lawn and driveway, looking like sinister lumps of coal.

We parked in silence and Lorenzo turned off the ignition. Opening my car door, I stepped out and immediately burst into sobs. Lorenzo came around to stand beside me.

Just then, a police cruiser pulled up, parking just below our steep driveway. It was one of our Westbank First Nation law enforcement officers (L.E.O.). Emerging, the L.E.O. scrutinized us for a few seconds. Seeing the tears streaming down my face, he remarked wryly, "Well, at least I know you're not looters, folks."

25

TIME TO FACE THE MUSIC

My first reaction to the cop's remark was, *How callous can you get?* But he turned out to be a nice guy.

"This is so weird for everyone." The officer cleared his throat. "I've been in my job for fifteen years and seen some doozies of wildfire damage in my time. But this takes the cake. It's like a law of randomness took hold here."

He pointed a finger, furrowing his brow at the pile of rubble across the street, lowering his voice like he was channeling the god Zeus on Olympus. "That house burns," he intoned. "The next one stays. The next one goes down…"

FINDING THE PHOENIX

The law of randomness seemed to determine whose houses burned...

I winced, glad our neighbours Steve and Tracy were not listening to this. But the man had a point. Our street was bizarre to contemplate. Trying to picture the wildfire raging through the neighbourhood, we had always envisioned it as completely wiped out. One goes—they all go. Looking through the binoculars above Westside Road showed otherwise. But the observers had been squinting through the lenses at a thick haze of almost impenetrable smoke, and so the visual information seemed unreliable.

Lorenzo was standing with the L.E.O., repeating "law of randomness" under his breath several times as they gazed around. Their voices receded into the background while I stared, mesmerized, at the charred pit that used to be Steve and Tracey's house.

Debris was strewn everwhere, except for two scorched Adirondack chairs in the front yard, perched side by side, bizarrely intact; as if waiting for someone to sit and crack open a beer. Looking to the left where the hillside trails began, I could see hundreds of giant ponderosa pines, standing grim and blackened, the needles a ghastly orange. Some listed against each other as if for support, others lay toppled to the ground, all the way down the mountainside.

It was like a battlefield, only with trees instead of people.

Burned trees on Bear Creek Road

So much woodland was burned I could see all the way down to Westside Road. For some reason this frightened me. The forest had been a buffer, a shield, a blanket of comfort and protection. Now it was gone, like a wall ripped away, exposing us to the cold, terrifying world.

For a moment I thought I'd been hurled into one of my deranged wildfire nightmares. But then I heard the cop and Lorenzo talking and I snapped out of it.

"This isn't going to be easy for you, folks…" the police officer was saying. He was overstating the obvious, but seemed so sincere I couldn't help liking him.

"That's true. It's already not easy," Lorenzo observed, without a trace of sarcasm. Preoccupied, his shoulders tense, he kept glancing at the front door. I knew he was itching to get in there and face whatever we needed to face. *The devil you know.*

"I'd like to warn you about a couple of things," the officer added. We looked at him, dubious. What could he need to warn us about besides the heartbreak of seeing what this fire had done to our neighbourhood?

"Looky-loos." He shaded his eyes with his hand and pointed down the road as if he could see a car approaching. "They're a pain in the butt. They're not allowed in here, and we'll try to keep them out, but they'll come anyway, usually on a Sunday drive. This is one of the hardest-hit neighbourhoods. People are going to be crazy curious to see it. You might feel invaded. Like monkeys in a zoo."

I thought of all the signs and caution tape surrounding the broken gate and melted fence. People would just barge through all that to gawk at houses burned to the ground?

Adrenaline coursed through me, and I stared down the street with narrowed eyes, as if it was already happening.

"We'll just ignore them," Lorenzo said in a stoic voice.

Speak for yourself, I thought, balling my hands into fists. Aloud, I asked through gritted teeth, "What else do we need to worry about?"

"Looters," the officer replied, looking disgusted.

I thought he was joking. "Looters?" I echoed, my voice rising. "In a burned-out neighbourhood. What would they have to loot?"

"You'd be surprised." (Fast forward a few days later, turned out he was right).

"Well," Lorenzo said, an edge in his voice, "thanks for all the tips, sir. Now I think we'd better take a look inside our house."

"Of course." The cop mock-saluted us. "Good luck, folks. Take care." He got in his car and drove off, passing a vehicle on its way up the hill.

It was Tim and Chantelle's car.

~

MY STOMACH CHURNED, and I looked instinctively at the yard next door. Broken glass littered the gaping front entrance. Yellow caution tape swathed the doorframe. From the look of the front, the rest didn't bode well. We hadn't gone inside our own home yet, let alone into the backyard, so we had no idea what either of ours looked like.

That their home was a burned-out shell inside had already been confirmed. But it wasn't yet clear whether the insurance company's report would deem their foundation sound. If so, they'd be forced to rebuild their house around it, instead of getting a whole new house like the other "total loss" residents. That would be the worst of both worlds.

Chantelle was the first out of the car, chestnut brown ponytail bobbing, flinging open the door of the passenger seat and propelling herself out sideways almost before Tim had stopped the car.

I broke into a jog as I hurried over, and we hugged. Lorenzo was right behind me. He walked over toward Tim, who was just getting out of the car. The look on his face seemed say that it was all just sinking in now.

"I wouldn't want to be facing this without you guys," Chantelle muttered in my ear. Her confiding tone reminded me of all the heart-to-heart talks we'd had on our hikes, delving into our similar pasts: dysfunctional families and the challenges of having to grow up before we were ready. The ongoing work of navigating happy and healthy lives with those we loved, despite all the loss and pain.

Now this wildfire. My throat threatened to close up, but I got hold of myself and gave her a reassuring hug.

"Same here. We'll face it together." I gestured to our house. "We haven't even been inside yet. Too busy having a meltdown and then talking to a cop warning us about looters and looky-loos."

It was the wrong thing to say. Chantelle's cheeks flushed.

"*Bastards! They'd better not dare!*" Her voice trembled with intensity. In retrospect this might seem like an overreaction, but at the time I understood it perfectly. There was so much pent-up emotion, and no one to blame for any of this. Future looters would have to do for now.

We'd been warned in advance about the state of Tim and Chantelle's place. But it was a different thing to behold the wreck of their home in real life, real time. The four of us gazed in bleak silence at the black gaping maw of their front door.

Looking through the doorway at the destroyed interior of Tim and Chantelle's home

So much caution tape, it was overkill. I felt like I was in a Stephen King movie. Chunks of broken glass and blackened embers were scattered around like horror-show confetti. The place didn't look exactly welcoming. But Chantelle folded her arms doggedly, then took a step toward the door closer; then another, with jerky movements, like she was being pulled forward by an invisible magnetic force.

Chantelle facing the haunting aftermath of the wildfire

"Watch for the glass—" I squeaked, looking at her bare toes peeking out of summer flip-flops.

"You can't go in there!" Tim said in a sharper tone as she continued toward the doorway. When she ignored him, he added, "That tape is there for a reason!"

Chantelle had stopped right in front of the doorway, poking her head between two pieces of tape to peer inside. At Tim's words, she straightened and defiantly swatted the layers of tape out of her way.

"I'm going in," she said flatly. "I don't care. It's my house."

Tim groaned. Chantelle shrugged. I grabbed her arm. "Wait!" I took off my sneakers. "You can't go walk around with unprotected feet. Let's trade shoes."

She nodded in agreement, and we quickly swapped footwear. Tim and Lorenzo were mumbling to each other in low voices, eyebrows furrowed. Probably talking about how crazy Chantelle was acting. But I knew how she felt. Sometimes you just need to know.

Chantelle's immediate goal was to find out if any of their belongings were salvageable. Like us, they had not believed for one minute the fire would reach our neighbourhood, and so had taken almost nothing with them.

As mentioned at the beginning, we'd packed the usual practical necessities of going away for the weekend. After the evacuation alert came, we'd grabbed documents, jewellery, a few favourite books and paintings. At the last minute, we'd also packed a few family photos that couldn't be reproduced, and objects that had sentimental value because they were connected with loved ones whom we'd lost (Lorenzo's mother, my son, Orion).

One photo was of Orion when he was two and a half, dressed as a firefighter. Everywhere we went during evacuation, I unpacked the picture and put it somewhere conspicuous, my bittersweet talisman against misfortune.

Orion

Talking to neighbours in the days to come, I gathered some random information about what they had taken.

Chantelle and Tim had grabbed Nash's favourite toys and some family photo albums. After finding out their home's interior was destroyed, she would agonize about what they'd left behind: her pampered house plants, Nash's aquarium, and cherished Christmas ornaments inherited from her late father. I had to keep reminding her that she'd been so fragile post-surgery it was a wonder she'd remembered anything.

Besides, she wasn't the only one. The majority of us had left almost everything behind.

Why take a bunch of clothes, furniture, dishes, books, sports equipment? When we would doubtless only be evacuated for a few hours at the most... Just long enough to go to the Hatching Post for a burger and a beer.

Or, even if we were evacuated for the whole weekend, no big deal. Just a minor inconvenience. We'd look back on it as an adventure, a hiccup in our summer. Within a few days we'd watch the smoke drift away, and the blue sky reappear, and then we'd go home.

A few days before we were allowed back to view our properties, I'd emailed back and forth with our strata President, Judith Harris, and she'd reminisced about their emotions during the first days of the evacuation.

...*We packed only one overnight bag and left at 3:00 pm to stay at our daughter's place in Summerland. When things went from bad to worse, it was a terrible shock, especially as residents began calling me to ask if I knew the status of their house. Or worse, to ask if it had burned down.*

Then, a neighbour texted me to say they had received a doorbell video from another resident showing the house next door to us was on fire, and they thought ours was as well. I was so devastated I wept all night.

Shortly thereafter, Mike and Mo sent me an email stating their doorbell video showed a house burning to the ground, and Mike thought it was Seagun's, but wasn't positive. He also thought his house was on fire because his doorbell video had suddenly stopped working. Right afterward, Seagun messaged me, asking if I'd heard anything about her house. I didn't have the heart to tell her what Mike had mentioned, in case it wasn't her home...

So much for our flippant assumptions that the wildfire 'thing' would be soon be over with, and all the panic and hassle would be a distant memory.

We'd been so arrogant in thinking we could predict the future.

∼

"Here goes," Chantelle announced, turning on her iPhone flashlight. She stepped gingerly over the threshold, glass crunching under her feet. Unable to stop myself, I crept up to the doorway, watching where I stepped. The smell of smoke and incineration was overpowering, but the air drifting from the doorway seemed cold.

Just beyond the threshold, I could see Chantelle's shadowy figure moving cautiously around, trying to get her bearing.

"Holy shit!" I heard her mutter.

"What?" Stepping across into the chilly darkness almost without being aware of it, a sharp pain in my heel snapped me back into reality. "Ow!" I bent down and pulled out a small shard of glass. Cursing myself for my idiocy after going to all the trouble of the shoe swap.

Chantelle's flashlight dazzled my eyes, causing me to cover my eyes with my arm. "Are you okay?" she asked.

"Yep. But why did you say, 'Holy shit'?" Her cell phone flashlight left my face, and she shone it in a big arc across the room.

I let out my breath in an explosive exhale. This room, in this house— a place I'd been inside many times—was unrecognizable.

Stumbling through the rooms, we ascended a mostly disintegrated staircase, pausing to take in a surreal sight: the master bedroom, pristine and unaltered , complete with several house plants that had somehow survived.

After staring, goggle-eyed, for a few seconds, we stepped into the adjoining bedroom (Tim's daughter Olivia's room when she stayed with them). This one looked entirely different. An operatic wreck of ash and cinders scattered across the bed's duvet and Olivia's small white piano.

Olivia's bedroom

The entire back of the house was also decimated; the hardest hit being Nash's bedroom, his playroom, his fish tank, and all his toys.

"It's like the universe pointed its giant finger at him and said, 'Pow, take that!'" Chantelle spoke in a shaky voice. "It's crazy. We can never tell him."

My shoulders felt like they'd been gripped with iron talons. If *their* place looked like this, what did *our* place look like inside? Were we in for the same horrible shock? After seeing the devastation in here, I wasn't sure I was strong enough to find out.

We wandered around a little more, but it was treacherous terrain, and gradually our morbid curiosity gave way to worrying about our own safety—parts of the floor and walls had collapsed, others looked like they were about to (not to mention the voices of our husbands calling for us to get the hell out of there).

We emerged, sooty and subdued, Chantelle clutching a couple of ferns and a prayer plant. She began loading them into the trunk, a look of grim triumph on her face.

A few meters away, Tim kicked at the roots of a burned shrub in their front yard. I was pretty sure he was crying. Awkwardly, I

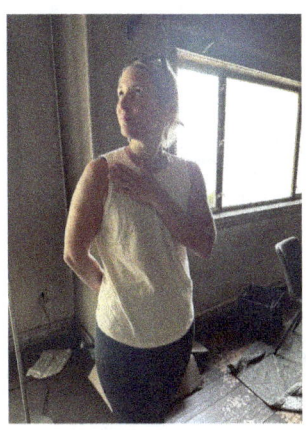
Chantelle in shock

moved blankets aside in the trunk, helping Chantelle arrange her plants. Tim looked over, shaking his head in disbelief. His expression, like a volcano ready to erupt, made me realize they needed time for a private conversation.

"Well," Chantelle said abruptly, as if her adrenaline tank had suddenly run out of fuel, "I guess that's enough for today. We're out of here." Hearing this, Tim walked toward us, moving like a robot.

I hugged her again as they went silently to either side of the car. "Bye," I said, trying to sound upbeat. "You saved some plants. It's a miracle!"

"Yup." She kept her eyes down as she opened the car door. "Good luck seeing your place…keep me posted…" Her voice trailed off and she shut the door. I watched as they drove away, my heart contracting with pity. Wishing I could have said something more than that inane comment about miracles. But, for some things, there are just no words.

Suddenly we were alone. Lorenzo and I stood in the driveway, looking at each other. No more stalling.

Time to go inside our house.

26

I WANNA GO HOME

When I was in elementary school, I learned to play the recorder. I'm dating myself, but there it is. We'd take our little flutey things out of their green velvet drawstring bags and proceed to commit a serious assault on our teacher's ears.

From the sheer force of nauseating repetition, I learned to hate some of the songs, but one of them stuck in my head like an ear worm: "Sloop John B," by the Beach Boys. Although I didn't understand most of the nautical references, the chorus moved me. It's a homesick, defiant refrain, ending with the line "I wanna go home…"

I sang that song to my babies when they were teething, not knowing why. It just kept popping up, like my subconscious mind was a jukebox and someone kept feeding it quarters.

That earworm had been playing off-and-on throughout this entire McDougall Creek wildfire ordeal. *I wanna go home.*

Now I *was* home. I was about to go through that doorway. But I didn't know what home was anymore.

And I was scared.

"This is so weird," I said. We were standing at the front door, and my knees were shaking. 'Knees shaking' is interesting to read and write about, but I don't enjoy it in real life. And it was something I hadn't experienced in a long while.

"Do you remember the code?" I asked Lorenzo, looking at the keypad. "Because I don't." I had a fierce impulse to turn and run down the hill. "And it might not even work, right?" I continued, giving a resigned shrug, as if we'd already tried and failed.

But Lorenzo just nodded, grabbing my hand as if he knew I might try to flee the scene. Without hesitation, he punched in the numbers, tapping briskly, and the familiar beep came.

We glanced at each other, and then Lorenzo pushed open the door and walked inside.

Everything looked the same.

A couple of mismatched sandals and a silky blue summer scarf were lying in the front entrance, the only clue that we'd left in a hurried panic.

But the plants in the foyer were deader than dead. Apparently the plant fairy hadn't come to our house and performed a miracle like it had to Tim and Chantelle's.

I berated myself for that thought. *Too bad a 'Your-house-escaped-the-wildfire' fairy hadn't come.* For them, for everyone in our neighbourhood whose place was obliterated. Thinking about it made me sick with guilt. I glanced at my face in the front entrance mirror, seeing it wan and white, eyes full of dread.

"Are you coming up?" Lorenzo asked. He had been gazing up the staircase and now looked at me over his shoulder, his eyes glittering with tension. I turned away from the mirror and hurried after him.

As we climbed the stairs, a foul stench wafted toward us. Hearing Lorenzo's muffled exclamation ahead of me, I knew it had hit him full force. It intensified as we neared the kitchen, becoming so putrid we covered our lower faces with our hands.

"Masks!" I hissed, suddenly remembering the notice advising us to wear them when we first entered our home.

I can only presume that, like us, everyone has a million masks left over from pandemic days. (You find them everywhere: drawers, closets, handbags, grocery bags. Sometimes it seems like they're procreating.) Anyway, I had hastily stuffed two masks in my small crossbody bag as we were leaving, and now I pulled them out.

Looking at each other masked up, I saw reflected in his eyes the same ironic thought as mine: *Haven't seen you like this in a while.*

We got to the top of the stairs. Inhaling, I almost gagged. The mask might help with toxic smoke particulates, but it was doing nothing to shield us from the malodorous reek that pervaded the upper floor. The living room, dining room, and kitchen all looked fine visually; but if you closed your eyes, you'd think we were standing on a giant mound of rotting garbage like in the movie *Slumdog Millionaire.*

Fast forward to the next day when we met with Shane, our assigned project manager from the restoration company. We were all wearing masks and trying not to retch. He told us they'd be doing a sponge test on the walls to determine the toxicity levels from the smoke.

We were stunned. "But we can't see anything," Lorenzo protested, gesturing around us. There's no sign of ash or soot. And we can't smell any smoke whatsoever!"

Shane shrugged and pulled a wry face. "It's because the toxic waste smell is so overpowering. Once we get the guys in the Hazmat suits in here and the fridges with the rotting food out of here, you'll smell the smoke, I guarantee it!"

This turned out to be true. And, astoundingly, there was a ton of ash and soot on all the surfaces, walls, floors, ceilings--invisible to the naked eye. It was scary to contemplate.

But on this day—our first homecoming—the only damage we could see inside the house was the slimy seepage of the fridge/freezer waste, which, besides being disgusting to look at, had destroyed a large portion of the floor.

We walked from room to room. Everything seemed

unchanged. But stepping out the back door was a different matter. Now *there* was some damage.

The fence separating our yard from Chantelle's was burned to a blackened crisp, and crumbling fast. Falling embers had scorched holes in our deck floor and hot tub cover.

Walking around the back yard, I leaned down and picked up something from a shrivelled, yellow patch of grass. It was an immense ember, looking like a lump of coal someone would spitefully leave in a Christmas stocking. A closer look at the lawn revealed countless more embers, pock-marking the grass like a plague.

Finding embers everywhere we looked, including this deck chair

I pictured the charred lumps in the air when they were alight, little missiles glowing a fiery orange, raining down from the blazing trees.

Marvelling again that our house was still standing. It seemed impossible.

Would I ever be able to look at my garden again as a blissful oasis? The blaze had decimated the front of our property—the hydrangea bushes and garden beds burned to the roots. An ugly, soul-parching thing to contemplate.

Worst of all was the silence. I was accustomed to an orchestra of birdsong in the back yard: quails, robins, magpies, jays, owls and ravens.

There wasn't a bird in sight.

We'd been wandering around in numb silence. Outside smelled way smokier, and the hills surrounding us were a dull and ugly rust colour. It was as if our house had landed somewhere it should not be.

We plodded heavily back to the front yard, just in time to see Steve and Tracy from across the street get out of their car and walk over to contemplate the pile of ashy debris that had been their home.

Steve and Tracy's house across the street

Our neighbours had their backs to us, and we approached them tentatively. "Hey." Lorenzo's voice was quiet, almost a whisper. They didn't turn around. I cleared my throat. They remained with their backs to us. Steve put his arm around Tracy, and her shoulders heaved silently. After another awkward moment, we retreated.

Time to go. Climbing into the car, we stared ahead, wordless. Lorenzo hunched over the steering wheel, and I slumped in my seat, pressing my fingertips together and wishing I'd brought my sunglasses. The late summer sun was beaming through the windshield. A month ago, we would have been basking in the warmth, but I winced away from it now. Heat and light reminded me too much of the enemy.

Plus, I was crying. Sunglasses would have come in handy.

We should have been able to unpack our bags and settle happily into our comfortable routines, like after every other time we'd been away from home. Instead, we were still evacuees, driving back to a temporary shelter, to regroup and wait for whatever came next.

Halfway down Mount Boucherie Road, we passed Quail's Gate winery, and I belatedly remembered I'd made dinner reservations there for tonight, because it was a special occasion.

No way were we going there now. I'd have to cancel.

I looked at Lorenzo, trying to keep the tremor from my voice. "Happy Anniversary, honey."

27

SURVIVORS' GUILT

Excerpt from *Castanet* Newspaper: Saturday September 2, 2023, 8:11 pm

The Central Okanagan Emergency Operations Centre said it doesn't expect to rescind any additional evacuation orders or alerts for the rest of the long weekend. In a statement, the EOC said crews will work through the long weekend to remove hazards and restore infrastructure so properties are safe for residents, noting this work is expected to take until early to mid-week.

"Returning residents to their homes safely and as quickly as possible remains a top priority. The areas where evacuation orders remain are those hardest hit by the fire and require more work before they are safe for residents to return," the statement said. "While crews are making good progress, they are dealing with challenging terrain that makes restoration more complicated."

∼

WAS this 2023 Labour Day long weekend stuck in a time warp? It seemed like it had lasted for a whole season.

Hunkered down at Jay and Jeanette's place, I couldn't relax. After seeing our home for the first time since evacuation, we'd been wrung out, and gone to bed early. But I'd been tossing and turning on the mattress ever since.

I finally gave up, and after much fumbling around, found the switch and turned on the bedside lamp.

Changing homes five times in the last month had necessitated memorizing different routes to the bathroom in the middle of the night, unfamiliar nightstands and light switch locations, and a subsequent propensity to bump into things in the dark.

"Not again..." mumbled Lorenzo, startling awake and throwing a hand over his eyes as the light hit him. I'd forgotten this one was so bright. Another thing about changing places so often.

"Sorry." I switched off the lamp and surreptitiously opened my iPad, Googling 'Survivor's Guilt,' a term Chantelle had mentioned when we first got the news that our houses were still standing. We'd been agonizing over those neighbour's houses which had been burned to the ground.

I think I'm coming down with 'Survivor's Guilt', Chantelle had texted, and I could almost feel her angst through the phone.

What's that?

But then I could hear Nash in the background yelling about not being able to find his soccer cleats.

Gotta go... she'd texted.

Flash forward to two weeks after Chantelle had discovered their house was also a *total loss*, and I was Googling "Survivor's Guilt" at 2:00 a.m.

The definition:

A response to an event where someone else experienced loss but you did not. Symptoms of 'Survivor's Guilt' or 'Survivor's Remorse' can be both psychological and physical, often mimicking those of PTSD.

Among the most common symptoms are feelings of helplessness, nightmares, flashbacks of the traumatic event, mood swings and angry outbursts, obsessive thoughts about the event, apathy and depression, difficulty sleeping.

Haha. I allowed myself a bleak chuckle at the realization that I had woken up to read about difficulty sleeping.

The man sleeping next to me, a faint smile on his face, had witnessed my mood swings and angry outbursts first-hand. Looking at him made me feel ashamed of my irritability, and I coined a new phrase: *Spousal Remorse.*

Lorenzo seldom got agitated about anything besides terrible drivers. But in recent days, I had noticed he was struggling with emotional swings of his own, especially after our brief return to the house. The other day he had put his arm around me as we walked with Oliver alongside the lake at dog-friendly Gellatly Park.

As I glanced at my husband, tears had filled his eyes out of nowhere. When I tried to say something, he had held up his hand, turning his face away. He didn't want to talk about it.

I thought about my nightmares, vivid and disturbing. In fact, *all* the symptoms listed online for Survivor's Guilt were the same as those for PTSD. Which I knew we already had.

Except for one: Guilt.

I AWOKE bleary-eyed to hear Lorenzo banging around our hosts' kitchen, looking for coffee mugs. Glancing at my phone, I saw it was 8:00. My nighttime Googling had made me sleep in well past the usual hour. Oliver looked at me hopefully from his dog bed. *Time to go out for a walk…?*

We still had no idea when it would be safe to return home. But our meeting with Shane from the restoration company was at 10:00 this morning. We were lucky he was meeting us on a Sunday of the Labour Day long weekend.

Mind you, this was not like any Labour Day weekend I'd ever seen—no tourists, no partying on the lake, no 'farewell summer-hello- fall' soirees at the wineries.

So back to our burned-out neighbourhood we went, this time

with Oliver in tow. As a valued member of our family, he needed to get accustomed to the unfamiliar landscape, not to mention all the other changes that were coming.

It wasn't as tough going in through the melted gate the second time, but it was still pretty bad. This time there was more activity on the street. At least six of our neighbours had pulled up in their vehicles and were milling around, looking dazed.

One of thirteen houses on our street that burned to the ground.

Chantelle and Tim had brought all the kids, both Nash and Tim's daughters Nya and Olivia; but not little Jax, because that puppy was way too hyper for the prevailing mood.

No one looked happy, but everyone flocked to Oliver, the superhero wildfire mascot.

Tim and Nash greet Oliver, the 'evacuation mascot'

Chantelle and Tim watched their kids with concern. Their faces had crumpled after seeing the house with its bashed in door and caution tape. I gave Chantelle a hug. "How are things looking? When are you getting it assessed?"

"Tuesday," she said, rolling her eyes. "But it'll be a tear-down for sure. It's gutted. There's no way that foundation is safe."

"So you'll get a new house, at least..." I tried to put enthusiasm in my voice. Seeing the look on her face, I had my first severe attack of Survivor's Guilt.

Why had I said that? *What was I thinking?*

She interrupted me before I could apologize. "It's coming from you..." She smiled. "You've been through this, too. Anyone else, and I might punch them in the nose."

And she probably would, I thought, grinning despite myself.

I spotted Raj walking up the path, looking lonely and dejected, her shoulders hunching forward beneath her white linen shirt. She twisted her thick black ponytail with nervous fingers.

"Hi Raj!" I nudged Lorenzo, and we hurried across the street. Everyone hugged, and then she knelt and petted Oliver, who enjoyed a polite acquaintance with their fluffy white little Bijon Frise, Ramu, and was surreptitiously looking around for him. Raj gestured at the burned-black cedar in their front yard, her shoulders stiffening.

We gazed at it, sombre. "Remember?" Raj murmured. "Watching it burn while I talked to you on the phone? And you told me to..." She looked at me with watery eyes.

"I told you to put down the phone and walk away." I paused. "You have to do that when you can't fix something. Or else the helpless feeling will just drive you crazy."

She gazed at me in silence, and I had the uncomfortable suspicion I was posturing, trying to come off as a philosophical guru, the way older people do when younger ones are in their listening orbit. "I just mean"... I stammered, "It was so hard watching our neighborhood burn down. In real time."

"So hard." Raj gave a deep sigh. "I'm glad my parents were away when it happened."

Raj's parents were not glad. Her dad Balaji had flown from India to Florida and joined his wife Sutha and her aging parents. But they ended up needing to stay longer because of ailing family members, and thus had missed the wildfire's dramatic appearance and the subsequent terrifying evacuation. Leaving their daughter to deal with everything that followed.

It's not like they would have wanted to endure that ordeal, but they hadn't wished for it to settle on Raj's shoulders. And now they were worried sick about their daughter. I got frequent texts from Sutha: *Is Raj okay? Does she seem stressed? Has she called the insurance people?*

She's okay, I would respond. I didn't reply to the second question, but it wasn't because I didn't know the answer.

Of course she was stressed! She was a 28-year-old woman (albeit brilliant and self-reliant, with a master's degree in epidemiology) left on her own to manage the family home and property. Then, with no warning, almost 50% of her neighbourhood burned down in a horrible rampaging wildfire. And she was evacuated.

Raj and other neighbours contemplating the stark reality of our burned homes

From her friend's house, she watched the live footage on the doorbell camera as flames licked greedily toward her house. And by some terrible stroke of timing, there were no other family members around. Not even her dog.

Regarding the third question: *Has she called the insurance people?*

Ah, the insurance people. All I'll say is that this topic would fill another book (which I'll never write, not being a total masochist).

∼

OTHER NEIGHBOURS WERE ARRIVING NOW, and we congregated in a loosely knit pack and began the tour of our desolate neighbourhood.

Beginning at the top of our street, from the line of brittle, charred ponderosa pines along the hillside, we ventured down to the bottom of the hill; where we gazed, wordless, at the melted fence and broken metal gate, and then turned to walk up the lower road, where the other half of the development was, ending back at the burned hillside.

Neighbourhood walkabout, like a funeral procession

The lower road properties have a more proximate view of Okanagan Lake, but I preferred our higher vantage point, where we could see the bridge lights strung across the lake like a diamond necklace at night, without even a hint of Westside Road traffic noise.

As we walked, we began chatting with some people we'd barely known before this happened, who were now our fellow sojourners on this wildfire odyssey. It reminded me of Life of Pi, with fire instead of water, and a road instead of a raft.

There was the husky, mustachioed owner of the second house on the east side of the lower road, who introduced himself as Ken. As we began down the lower road, he stopped, arms folded, in front of the smoking remnants of his home. Little keepsakes—teapots and vases—had been carefully perched on the scorched bricks of their front wall.

Talking to each other was a lifeline for people in our traumatized neighbourhood

Ken pointed at them, lips quivering, and then seemed embarrassed by his display of emotion. "Call me 'Crybaby Ken,'" he joked, but no one laughed.

As we continued walking down the road, I had an impulsive thought. I voiced it to Ken. "I'm thinking of writing a memoir about our evacuation. Is it okay if I mention you?" Saying it recklessly, not sure if I meant it. I was way behind on publishing the third book in my fantasy fiction trilogy. It would be crazy to switch to non-fiction. *If only this was fiction,* I thought fiercely. *I could change all of it with the snap of a finger.*

"You can put me in the book," answered Crybaby Ken, "No problem."

I had a surge of energy I hadn't felt in a long time. I didn't entirely comprehend it. But the thought of writing a memoir about this, capturing people's emotion in a crisis of such proportions...it gripped me with a sense of purpose. And, hey, it would be one way of dealing with survivor's guilt...

'Crybaby' Ken stands in front of his burned-out shell of a home

28

ONE MONTH GONE

Excerpt from *Castanet* Newspaper, Monday September 4th

The battle to snuff out the McDougall Creek wildfire continues on a long weekend Monday. The BC Wildfire Service reported increased fire activity on Sunday because of a weather inversion, which led to smouldering ground fire growth on the weekend. Despite modest precipitation, the potential for fire behaviour to increase Monday remains.

We were deflated to realize that Labour Day weekend was coming to a close, and the fire was still a threat. I'd kept thinking there was some 'September Clause' that I could invoke...

But then we got some news that cheered us right up.

Pierre and Colleen were back in town! They had driven in from Edmonton and were staying at the Towne Place Hotel in Westbank. We went and hung out in their hotel room. Knowing Colleen was vegetarian, I brought them homemade eggplant parmesan. Drinking gin and tonics while heating the casserole, we reminisced in increasing intensity and volume about *evacuation day*.

"Remember we were going to go out on our boat that afternoon?" Colleen shook her head. "And drink rosé? And order pizza to be delivered when we tied up to the dock on Water Street?"

"I'd really been looking forward to that..." I rubbed my eyes. It seemed like years ago we had made those plans.

Pierre stood up. "That's it," he yelled. "Come on!" When we stared at him, he gestured to the door. "Enough with our little pity party. Both our houses are still standing. Yes, we know there's damage and we're probably going to hear about a lot more. But still. They're standing. And we're here for those neighbours whose houses aren't. But we have to forget about this for a few hours. Let's head over to Whiski Jacks. We're going dancing!"

Dancing our troubles away at Whiski Jack's in Westbank

PIERRE AND COLLEEN SCHAAF were wonderful neighbours who had become even more wonderful friends. They lived in Royal

Heights only part time but had a positive influence that resounded full-time.

Pierre and Colleen boosting morale.

Pierre had been instrumental in extending Royal Height Properties' lease with the Westbank First Nation to 125 years, raising its appeal as a place to live and simultaneously upping the owners' property values. A retired nurse, Colleen had taken on the task of Social Director on the strata council. Her fun-loving but nurturing outlook was the best of both worlds.

One week to the *day* before the wildfire ravaged our development, the Schaafs had hosted a backyard potluck barbecue everyone in Royal Heights Properties. It was a blast— a beautiful summer evening spent with neighbours we had become fond of, along with others we were just getting to know. I couldn't think about it now, recalling all the smouldering destruction that happened only a week later, or I would start weeping and maybe never stop.

Instead I kept dancing—with Colleen at this particular moment. Even now, during this wildfire crisis, she took her social directing duties seriously.

"It's especially important during this time!" she shouted in my ear, as we jived around the dance floor at Whiski Jack's. "We need to get together and raise our collective morale!"

Which was why they were hosting another neighbourhood get together tomorrow morning. In their backyard just like before, but this time with bottled water and soft drinks only. No celebratory feast.

Nothing to celebrate.

THE NEXT MORNING, Raj joined us as we made our way down the hill to the Schaaf's house. Contemplating Pierre and Colleen's parched front lawn was dispiriting. But, as we walked along the side of the house to the back yard, it got worse.

They had a beautiful arbour, a summer haven where I had sat blissful and content, imagining I was back in Italy. Usually festooned with lush and purple ripening grapes in the summer, it was barren now. There were no grapes, only brittle vines hanging in forlorn strands from the blackened wood.

It was apparent their backyard foliage had suffered more than ours had, probably because the house next door (Mo's and Mike's) had burned to the ground, one of the more dramatic conflagrations, if you listened to the firefighters' talk. A wave of disorientation struck me, mingled with a sharp pang of grief.

And suddenly I spotted Mo. Neighbourhood buzz had proved correct. She was indeed pregnant; palms cradled protectively over her belly as she sat in a lawn chair, her back turned away from their burned property.

Mo refused to look around the whole time we were there. "That's where I lived," she would greet each person as they arrived, pointing back over her shoulder while gazing straight ahead. "That was my house." Now and then she would add (unnecessarily) "It's gone now."

The girl was clearly in a state of shock. Mike wasn't with her, being out of town on business, but Colleen hovered like a mother hen. I didn't know her well enough to provide any real comfort, but I offered enthusiastic congratulations on their pregnancy, and her face brightened a little.

I was tempted to try and cheer Mo up by remarking they might have a new house built by the time the baby was born--with a brand-new nursery. But I didn't know whether that would be the case (turned out it wasn't) or even whether they planned on staying in Royal Heights. And I was afraid to ask.

An unspoken etiquette had arisen around discussing the wildfire. No one whose house *hadn't* burned down asked people whose house *had* burned whether they were rebuilding and staying here; or taking the other option of an insurance payout and leaving this wildfire-wrecked neighbourhood in the rear-view mirror.

Instead, people discussed four things: What they had been doing when they got the evacuation order. What stuff they had taken with them when they fled their homes. Where they had gone. Where they were now.

There were some interesting answers:

The "Three Musketeer" couples, as I secretly thought of us (Lorenzo and I, Chantelle and Tim, Pierre and Colleen) had all been home, texting each other incredulously about being evacuated from a wildfire that none of us had even heard of until a couple of hours prior.

Dan and Mariana were also here. A good thing, because Dan was the one who manually wrangled our neighbourhood's malfunctioning electronic gate open for the fire department to get in, and the last few residents to get out.

Raj was here. But of course, her parents were still in Florida, biting their nails. As if she knew I was thinking about her, she came up to stand beside me, wearing a tremulous smile that belied her red-rimmed eyes.

Knowing she missed her parents and her dog Ramu, I squeezed her hand. "Your mom's coming tomorrow!" I reminded her. "We'll go for a walk in Kalamoir Park, and then for coffee at Lakeside Coffee Shop." She nodded, but her gaze was dragged like a magnet toward the pit that had been Mike and Mo's place.

People were mingling more now, and I talked to other neighbours who had been absent when our RHP was evacuated.

For instance, Nora and Ross McConnell from #21 (on the lower street of the cul de sac) were at a Blue Rodeo concert in Kamloops when the evacuation alert came.

It was Nora's birthday when she heard the news. Her blue eyes swam with tears as we stood reminiscing in the Schaafs' back yard. She told me that the year before, also *on her birthday*, her husband Ross had suffered a heart attack. Thankfully he'd recovered, as he demonstrated by standing beside her and listening solemnly while she talked. But still, what a scare.

And now the wildfire evacuation. "No more birthdays for me!" Nora said bitterly.

"Don't say that!" I answered. It was a casual remark, but superstition seized me. "You'll have lots more birthdays!" I exclaimed, and Ross nodded emphatically.

I found myself entwined in a long conversation with Nora, who was speaking softly, ignoring the constant stream of tears trickling down her cheeks. "I still can't believe this," she kept saying. "Our house is gone."

"But *we're* still here," Dan said. He had walked up to us unnoticed. "Sorry to interrupt," he added. "But sometimes I need to remind myself of that fact. If you think about it, it's a miracle that not a single person died in this wildfire. Remember Maui a few weeks ago? They weren't so lucky."

It was true. We all stood in silence. Behind me I could hear Mo's plaintive murmur, telling someone else about the house next door that used to be there. She was going to be a mother soon, and she was ok, her husband was ok, her unborn baby was okay. It was something we shouldn't take for granted.

Nora stared at Dan, then wiped her bloodshot eyes. "You're right," she said. "Thank you."

Ross put his arm around her shoulders. "We'll get going now," he told us. "This is a bit much for her." I gave her a hug and got permission to put her in my memoir—if I ever wrote it. It might be too sad to recount. I decided not to overthink it.

Most of our other neighbours didn't stay very long at the Schaaf's backyard gathering that afternoon. But those who lingered began to relax a bit. By relaxing, I mean felt free to burst into spontaneous tears. Clutching on to our bottles of Bubbly water, we mingled in a disjointed way, exchanging stories and venting emotions.

It's actually not as bad as it sounds.

"Where are Steve and Tracy?" someone asked. I think it was Raj, still haunted by the doorbell camera footage of their house burning down. She couldn't unsee the image of the huge ember flying from their roof and igniting the tree in her front yard. Also, her house had survived while Steve and Tracy's had not. Survivor's guilt had tracked her down.

Colleen told us Steve and Tracy were out house hunting today. We stared, flabbergasted. "They're not going to rebuild here?" Lorenzo asked, incredulously.

"Yup, you bet they are," Pierre answered over his shoulder, rooting around in the cooler for another can of soda water. "But they know it'll take a long time. So they decided to pull the trigger and buy another house in the meantime. That way, Tracy's parents can have some stability. Poor folks, they've been pretty discombobulated."

As the cliché goes: Drastic times sometimes call for drastic measures. (Fast forward to a year later: Steve and Tracy's new house still wasn't complete. Mike and Mo's was also still in the construction stage. Nora and Ross decided not to return to RHP).

∽

LATER THAT NIGHT, after we'd left Pierre Colleen's, we sat on Jay and Jeanette's deck, watching the full moon's silver light reflected in the still waters of the lake. We raised our glasses to them in an appreciation toast for all the support and appreciation they'd given us.

In a recent talk with Jeanette, she'd confided that she'd broken down in tears a few times from survivor's guilt. They had other friends who'd been devastated by the fire; including a couple we knew, Ed and Debbie, whose house was unfortunately right next door to Okanagan Lake—gone now, like it had never existed after the fire had rampaged down Westside Road like an avenging monster...

I told her not to feel guilty. But I think my words sounded a bit hollow. It's easier said than done, as I knew from experience.

With Jeanette and Jay a few weeks before the wildfire hit.

I thought again about what Dan had said. *We're all still here. No one died.*

West Kelowna Fire Chief Jason Brolund had recently disclosed to the public that Canada Task Force 1 had taken dogs to search hundreds of suspected sites where people might have stayed behind, despite evacuation orders.

"Thankfully, they found no casualties," Brolund said in a heartfelt voice. He leaned forward over the podium and closed his eyes for a few seconds. For the first time since the wildfire began, I thought he might break down in tears. But he straightened up again and smiled steadily at the camera. "It's very encouraging for all of us involved in this."

And Chief Brolund didn't just have the residents to worry about—As he later told me, he had his own team: the West Kelowna Fire Department—his work family— who were on the front line, facing the real danger. Throughout the wildfire crisis, there wasn't a day he didn't wake up without being haunted by the fear of losing one of them.

Not for the first time, I thought of all the firefighters who had risked their lives to battle this terrifying monster, battling to save our community. Any one of them could have succumbed to the fire—in any number of ways. There was danger all around. It was a Finding the Phoenix moment.

No one had died.

29

HANGING ON

Excerpt from *Global News*, **September 14, 2023 (Kathy Michaels, 4:09 pm)**
In the aftermath of the McDougall Creek wildfire, 27 kilometres of power lines, 426 poles and 66 other pieces of equipment needed to be replaced...

Burned poles and other equipment took months to be replaced

It was mid-September, and our neighbourhood remained off-limits. Almost every other affected area in West Kelowna had been given the green light for owners to return to their properties.

After a month of being evacuated, we were beyond tired of living in other people's houses. But our gratitude prevented us from voicing it, even to each other. The subtle indications were there, though. One of us would fumble through a cupboard, trying to find something, or trip over an unexpected obstacle; and then sigh, loud enough for the other one to hear.

When we were out and about in our community and ran into other people, the talk centered on when the wildfire would finally be designated as 'in control'. Which of course was an entirely different thing from 'being held.' Several times, the winds had changed, and the blaze was a looming threat again.

It was like being kept in captivity by a bad-tempered toddler with a flame-thrower.

We met with our restoration guy again, and he explained they were putting 'air-scrubbers' into our house in anticipation of us returning home.

"It'll take at least a couple of weeks to clean the air of toxins," Shane said, gesturing with a flourish to the huge rectangular boxes being set up throughout the house. One of the technicians flipped a switch, and a sound began that resembled a jet engine firing up before take-off.

I put my hands over my ears, staring at him in disbelief. "A couple of weeks?" I yelled, to make myself heard over the roar.

Oliver dived under the dining room table, where he lay, quaking with fear. He didn't like the sounds of the vacuum cleaner or blender either, but this was worse.

"How many hours a day do these things need to be running?"

"Twenty-four hours a day. And don't turn them off!" Shane snapped his chewing gum for emphasis. "But you won't have to worry about the noise for a while—you won't be living here, remember? You're not allowed home yet."

Oh, yeah, I thought bitterly. *What a relief.*

∽

LYING IN BED THAT NIGHT, I got a text from Chantelle:

I'm so worried about what we're going to do when we have to check out of the Eldorado Hotel. I feel like I'm going to have an anxiety attack. We've only got a few days left here. I'm desperate to feel grounded somewhere. Been reaching out to

all the house rental ads on Facebook, but either they don't reply, or are only willing to do short-term lease, which won't work for us.

Survivor's guilt gnawed away at me. *Can I phone you later?*

Of course, and no need to call back today. Just checking in because I miss ya that's all...

Feeling sick, I scrolled through my contacts, searching for someone that might be able to rent their place to Chantelle's family. The house would have to be a fair size, because Tim's teenage daughters lived with them part-time. And the rental market in Kelowna was brutal, with almost a zero-rate of availability at any given time.

There was no one. I vowed to keep my eyes and ears open, though, and sent a text to Daria to check on the hospital website for available housing. It was the least I could do for my neighbour—my friend.

While I was whining about my torched hydrangeas and wringing my hands about when we'd be back into our place, Chantelle and Tim were facing a year or more of being evacuated, and scrambling to find a more permanent place before their seven-year-old boy started school.

I had begun to notice something about our Royal Heights Properties neighbours, though. No one whose house had burned down seemed mad at us for not sharing the identical tribulations as them. We were all just commiserating together about the wildfire disaster that had hit us out of the blue. About how we were coping with it.

Come to think of it, deep down I wasn't really mad at anyone either. I'm talking about those people who hadn't been here for any of it. Even if they sometimes said the wrong things. It wasn't their fault this calamity had happened, or that they got confused about timelines and locations. Most of them cared about us and wanted to help.

My irritation level was receding as I found more Finding the Phoenix moments. Nobody had a road map for what we were going through. But as long as we kept our minds and our hearts open, we could get through this.

Sappy, but true.

But while I wrestled somewhat successfully with my see-sawing emotions during the day, trying to accentuate the positive and nurture my small flame of optimism, nighttime was a different matter. I continued to struggle with my wildfire dream demons.

∼

LITTLE STRAW HOUSES NIGHTMARE

I am high above the ground, hovering in the sweltering summer air. Looking down, I glimpse something unexpected and picturesque: a village of tiny cottages, clustered close together. Huts made of wicker or straw. They are so quaint. Are they dollhouses? Squinting to see better, I suddenly realize they look dry, flammable, even...

Drifting down a little, I look closer, becoming worried, because I spot mounds of shredded newspaper on the cottage floors. Why is it there? It makes no sense...

And then I see little people, far below, walking all around. The houses aren't dollhouses, they're real houses. And they're going to burst into flames at any moment, but no one realizes it. The villagers are oblivious. Not one tiny person in any of the tiny houses knows what is going to happen.

"Wake up!" Lorenzo's voice cut through my dream, and I sat upright with a jolt, staring at him with wild eyes.

"I was so scared," I told him. "My heart is still pounding..."

"*You* were scared?" He held up his hands as if to shield himself. "*I* was scared. You were slapping at me like you were trying to put out a fire."

∼

THE NEXT MORNING I was still shaking off the remnants of my nightmare, like picking pieces of straw out of my hair, when Raj texted me, sounding exuberant for the first time since the day of the evacuation. It was like a breath of fresh air.

Her mother, Sutha, was finally back from Florida. They'd made a flurry of arrangements: Raj had moved out of her friend's place, and she and Sutha had rented an Airbnb in Lakeview Heights, near Kalamoir Regional Park. Their little doggy Ramu was back, so things were brightening up a little bit for Raj.

We can finally go for that walk along the lake, Judith...

It was a beautiful morning. Late summer in the Central Okanagan is breathtaking. Why? The seasons are more moderate than elsewhere in B.C.'s interior. Colours are richer, and even when it's hot there's shade to be had. In Kalamoir Park, there are twenty-eight hectares of spectacular beachfront trails, winding through wooded black cottonwood groves. The delicate Mariposa lily flaunts its blossoms, and prickly pear cacti peek up from the gritty soil, brittle but gorgeous.

Wildflowers flourish in Kalamoir Regional Park

Wildlife abounds (there's an owl that everyone claims is *their* owl) deer, coyotes, and bears. Keep your dogs on leash, unless you descend from the main path onto one of the designated off-leash "Bowser Beaches," in which case your pooch can let 'er rip...

In mid-September, the leaves are just beginning to be tinged with the vibrant hues of fall—crimson, golden yellow, and vivid orange—but it's still green and fresh everywhere. Except if a wildfire has paid a recent visit.

Have I mentioned I *love* Kalamoir Regional Park?

Being on the other side of Highway 97, this pocket of West Kelowna (Lakeview Heights) had been spared from the McDougall Creek wildfire. Meeting at the lake trail, we all took a moment to soak in the cobalt blue, silver-flecked waters of Okanagan Lake.

Sutha gave me a warm hug, her cocoa brown eyes glowing. I asked her why she looked so serene. She explained her source of joy: It was Ganesh—the Hindu god who takes the form of an elephant— who had saved their home. Looking quietly proud, she revealed she kept a small shrine of Ganesh in their yard. It was tucked away just to the left of their front door, behind a small stone fountain. I had seen the fountain before on several occasions but somehow missed the shrine.

I was touched by the thought of a cherished spiritual relic. "I can't believe I didn't see it before..." I began.

She held up a hand, waving away my apology. "Judith, listen to what I am saying! This is a wonderful story!"

Not wishing to appear disrespectful, I nodded my head, waiting. Sutha smiled. "It has always been my habit to leave offerings at the shrine every day," she told me. "And this time it paid off!"

Sutha went on to relate that the flames had come so close to their door they had scorched the little metal god. ("It was bad! I will show you, Judith!") The wildfire had burned some of their trees to the ground, and embers had bombarded their house and yard like fiery little comets, doing a ton of damage. But their home still stood.

Sutha was convinced that Ganesh had 'taken one for the team' and shielded their house from the blaze.

Throughout her mother's recitation, Raj remained respectfully silent, which didn't surprise me. I already knew that although she was hip and educated, she was also very devout.

All at once, I recalled the police officer who had stopped at our house the day we were first allowed back, and his words about "the law of randomness."

Everyone had a theory, and our belief systems helped us hang on...

WE CONTINUED OUR LAKE WALK, doggies Oliver and Ramu ambling companionably just ahead of us, nosing at the shrubs and marking their territory in tandem.

All at once a family of quail startled out of a nearby bush, bolting in their customary panicked way right across our path. They were fleeing as if the seven hounds of hell were pursuing them, instead of two bumbling dogs who just gaped at them in confusion. The chicks were so tiny—not even as big as a hen's egg. But their little twiggy legs were a blur as they fled for their lives. They were so cute.

Raj giggled at the sight. I nudged her, smirking. "I bet we looked like that when we were evacuating from the wildfire..."

Her smile faded, and I thought, *too soon...*

In truth, making wildfire evacuation jokes was too soon for me as well. My recent nightmare about the straw houses and tiny scurrying people had insinuated its way into my waking imagination. Dark thoughts plagued me about how fragile and helpless we humans are in the grand scheme of things.

Admittedly, I often manage anxiety by funneling it into humour—it's sometimes an inappropriate coping mechanism, I know.

But it beats jumping off a bridge.

30

BEING HELP

Excerpt from *CBC News*, September 22, 2023

McDougall Creek wildfire is classified as "being held" but it remains a wildfire of note, meaning it continues to be highly visible and/or presents a threat to public safety.

"The response to a fire of this scale requires strong teamwork and collaboration across jurisdictions," an online statement by the B.C. Wildfire Service said.

Officials say an area restriction order, limiting who can travel to the vicinity of the fire, will remain in place until at least October 3. Those allowed through include firefighters, people with homes in the area that are not under evacuation order, and people doing agricultural activities.

Almost all remaining evacuation orders issued for the City of West Kelowna have been rescinded, with the exception of a handful of properties.

It was official.

After a month of being evacuated, we had finally gotten the news that we could go home. But it felt strange, unreal. In some ways...wrong.

"But you can wait, folks!" Shane reminded us. Our restoration manager was weighing in as if he was a personal friend. "If you're staying someplace comfortable, then what's the rush? Remember, the air scrubbers are still there. And those goddamn things are goddamn noisy."

We laughed. Shane had a way of putting things.

His words recalled a vivid dream I'd had the night before; where the air scrubbers were not big square boxes, but crazy hands with bright yellow rubber gloves, roaring noises emanating from the fingertips as they zipped all over the house, scouring the walls, snapping their fingertips on the ceilings and floors, and slapping their palms against the windows.

"It might not be comfortable yet," I muttered to Lorenzo. "The air scrubbers…"

He raised his eyebrows. "Every day that we've been gone, you've lamented about it. About how long we've been out of our home. How you'd give anything to sleep in your own bed."

I opened my mouth to protest. He held up a hand. "Sweetie, I'm not calling you a complainer. I feel exactly the same way." His voice broke, just a little, as he looked at me. "And now we *can*. Move back home." He gestured around us. "Sleep in our bed. I can't believe you're hesitating!"

We were standing in the master bedroom, staring down at a giant pile of clothes that the dry cleaners had just dropped off.

This was yet another thing we never could have imagined would result from the wildfire damage. *All* our clothes and bedding, draperies, towels, area rugs, etc. had to be professionally dry cleaned to get rid of the carcinogenic smoke toxins. Insurance covered it, thankfully, but it was a hassle when we discovered batches of our clothes mysteriously went missing, especially the expensive ones like Lorenzo's business suits, and the leather jacket he had bought me in Florence, Italy, on our honeymoon.

Ah, well. I gave an inward sigh. *First world problems…*

I was discovering an additional unpleasant side effect of survivor's guilt: Forbidding myself from getting upset over "little" things. Which meant anything that didn't include *our home burning to cinders.* There was always a stern inner voice admonishing me, saying, *Don't you know how lucky you are?*

But maybe that was a good thing—wasn't there a whole series of self-help books called "Don't Sweat the Small Stuff"?

I ran my fingers over my favorite navy-blue wool turtleneck, which I wouldn't be wearing for another six months. It looked brand new after a trip to the cleaners. Not everything was doom and gloom....

Lorenzo cleared his throat. He was gazing at me, arms folded, and I realized he was still waiting for me to answer.

I shrugged. "We can talk about it more back at Jay and Jeanette's. Right now, let's get these things hung up. And I need to find my Lulu Lemon tights. I'm sick of wearing the same workout clothes every day."

After sifting through our clothes, we surveyed our new fridges and freezers, which workers had just installed, then watered the lawn, in a despondent, "too little, too late" kind of way.

After that, I walked Oliver up and down our burned and deserted street, looking in vain for any other neighbours who might somehow be around.

Solitary walk with Oliver down our post-apocalyptic street

I kept thinking about Lorenzo's words as we stood contemplating yet another ceiling-high mountain of plastic-batched drycleaning dumped on our bed:

"Sweetie, I'm not calling you a complainer...I feel exactly the same way..."

My throat had clogged up, making hard to swallow. I'd begun crying without realizing it. The lake had become nothing but a blue blur through my tears. I found myself somehow on my knees on the sooty asphalt, my fingers buried in Oliver's fur; on a deserted, ashy street that used to be so, so beautiful.

Trying to remember any other time since our evacuation day that that I'd heard terms of endearment from my husband. Or the last time we'd hugged each other, outside of terror or relief hugs.

I couldn't remember a single time.

Lorenzo and I looking at the lake at the beginning of the summer

Chores done, we locked up. Even with the doors closed, we could hear the air scrubbers behind us as they continued their vigilant scouring. We climbed in the car and headed back to our latest refuge.

As we drove through the Royal Heights gate, I glanced at the charred trees and melted fence, cringing at the thought of encountering this sight every day, sometimes multiple times a day. Would we eventually get used to it?

Which brought me to the bigger question: How long would it take to restore our neighbourhood to some semblance of normal? If ever…

FOR THE SECOND time that summer, we were sitting by the pool at Jay and Jeanette's place, sipping rosé and watching Daria and Sean play with Maya in the water, while Oliver hovered anxiously on the deck, never taking his eyes off our five-month-old granddaughter. It was funny and cute—the way he didn't entirely trust any of us humans to take care of the baby.

Daria and Sean and Maya visit us at Jeanette and Jay's

"When are you guys going home?" Daria called out. "Your friends are back from Vancouver soon, aren't they?"

It was true. Jay and Jeanette were driving back from the coast the day after tomorrow. They had told us that even after they came home, we could continue to stay in their Airbnb (quaintly named "Quail's Nest.")

I was waving a toy mermaid at Maya and didn't answer. "When are you guys going home?" Daria repeated.

"It's up to your mom," Lorenzo answered, shooting me a pointed look.

Earlier that morning, I had gone into the back yard and picked ripe cherry tomatoes from Jeanette's lovingly tended vegetable garden. Now I reflected on how much I missed my own small garden, which had somehow escaped the fire's wrath.

There were tomatoes, and peppers, eggplants and herbs, all waiting to be picked and thrown into a giant pot of pasta sauce in my kitchen. And I knew exactly where to find all the utensils.

Some garden bounty escapes the wildfire

It was time to get off the fence.

"We're going home tomorrow," I told Daria.

Maya slapped the water with her chubby little hands as if in celebration. We all burst out laughing at the coincidence.

Through the laughter, I felt my shoulders begin to tremble. The fear of going home still clung to me. Things would not be the same. Ever.

But life doesn't wait for us while we endlessly wring our hands because of the changes that hit us. It just keeps going. I felt ready to face the next chapter.

31

PICKING UP THE PIECES

Excerpt from the *Revelstoke Review*, October 5th, 2023
MCDOUGALL CREEK WILDFIRE IN WEST KELOWNA UNDER CONTROL

The McDougall Creek wildfire is now under control after burning for almost two months.

After being held for two weeks, the fire is now under control, according to B.C. Wildfire Services.

This means that, due to suppression efforts, the blaze will not spread any further. Additionally, all remaining evacuation orders and alerts were rescinded on Thursday, September 28th. Central Okanagan Emergency Operations has also ended the local state of emergency.

We had been home for a couple of weeks. It was strange to be almost the only people back on our street—like being in a ghost town. All that was missing was a bunch of tumbleweeds blowing down the street. I tried my best not to dwell on the forsaken atmosphere that pervaded Royal heights Properties.

Besides, there was so much to deal with, it was overwhelming.

For instance, at this moment I was sneezing violently from being in proximity to heaps of fire-damaged spices and condiments that needed to be itemized for replacement by the restoration company.

Hundreds of household items were deemed too toxic to keep or use, and restoration company employees trod continually in and out of the house, removing boxes of damaged goods or returning yet more bags of dry cleaning. They were polite and cheerful, and I did my best to respond in kind. Even so, it was annoying and intrusive, and the discordant noise of the air scrubbers did little to soothe my jangled nerves.

I sneezed for the umpteenth time and then wandered into the backyard to take a break. Oliver followed at my heels, indulging in a favourite pastime of his by rolling around in the cool grass.

Lorenzo had disappeared into the garage a couple of hours ago, and I knew he was on the phone arguing with the insurance people (something he would spend the best part of the next year doing on an almost daily basis). The 'squeaky wheel gets the grease' is the perfect adage for dealing with insurance companies. Often it seemed like we were talking to walls of stone, and that nothing would ever get done. And there was so much to be done…

Other neighbours were facing their own challenges. Aleda and Joseph from #1 got their ghastly car skeletons towed away in a bizarre, rusty, parade down our mostly deserted street.

Aleda and Joseph's burned vehicles

FINDING THE PHOENIX

Burned cars being towed from our street

Astoundingly, Joseph and Aleda's speedboat had survived the fire. But the cop's prediction about 'looters' proved correct when police arrested thieves trying to actually steal it from their burned-out, roped-off property. I can still get worked up about that. Some people...

The prediction about 'looky-loos' came true as well, and I have to admit I did my share of glaring and mouthing hostile imprecations at intruders who drove slowly up and down our street, taking pictures and pointing at the carnage with thrilled expressions. I was especially incensed at the people who parked in front of Steve and Tracy's former house.

On one occasion, a woman got out of her car and walked into their yard, looking like she was about to sit in one of the Adirondack chairs and take a selfie. When I shouted out to her, outraged, she waved at me, much like I was—you guessed it—a monkey in a zoo, and snapped a pic.

I was finally cured of this hyper-reactive surliness after one time too many of doing my "Madwoman of McDougall Creek wildfire" routine. Outside watering the Japanese maple, one of the only plants in the front yard that had survived, I saw a vehicle approaching the top of the hill, slowing down, the driver pointing, and his passenger videoing the burned houses with her phone. I let the hose go, wildly spraying everywhere, and shook my fist at the vehicle.

"What are you looking at??" I yelled, and the people turned to me, eyes wide with shock.

They were friends of ours, dropping by for a visit.

CHANTELLE AND TIM had found a house in nearby Rose Valley, with a pool no less, which overjoyed Nash and the girls. It was a huge relief, as school had started.

But unfortunately, the latest news about their house was the worst case scenario they had dreaded. Their insurance company had deemed the foundation to be sound, and so they would have to rebuild around it. They were already girding up for what would be a prolonged battle to get things done correctly. But, like all of us, they were taking things one day at a time.

Dan and Mariana had moved back into their home, next door to us on the other side. We compared notes and realized we had a similiar amount of damages.

The wildfire had wreaked so much damage that hadn't been visible at first. Our insurance claim had a staggering total—to the tune of $200,000.

Among other things, our roof needed replacing, along with the gutters, deck, front yard landscaping, outdoor lighting, all outdoor deck and lawn furniture, and on and on. And no item was too small to bicker over. It was astonishing to discover that our insurance company was better than most.

OBLIVIOUS TO THE looming spectres of insurance claims and looky-lous, Oliver continued to roll in the cool grass, which was finally springing back to life, moist and velvety green.

The backyard looked beautiful compared to the desecrated front of the house; and I felt myself relaxing into an almost tranquil state, soothed by watching my carefree pooch and listening to the quail family rustle and twitter in the shrubbery.

I couldn't wait for Chantelle to be back, and little Jax to slip through his secret hole in the fence, raising our spirits with his puppy vibes. But it was going to be a long while till that happened.

Oliver and Jaxx cavorting in the backyard before the fire hit

Not for the first time since returning home, I wondered where the stellar jays were. Had they fled the burning hillside, never to return? The thought made my eyes smart with tears, which I blinked away, angry at my weakness. I stared at the fence beside the hot tub right below the mountain ash tree.

This was where the glorious, resplendently blue jays would gather, waiting for conversation and the odd peanut.

I stared harder. Willing them to appear.

Wishing more than anything to hear my jaunty little birds summon me in the mornings, like before. To go out in my housecoat, pockets lined with peanuts, and offer them their daily snack; while they gazed at me in a shrewd but friendly fashion with their beady black eyes.

But I hadn't seen the brilliant blue flash swooping down since the day we were evacuated. I recalled vividly how that afternoon it had seemed like Stella was trying to warn me about something.

Thinking these thoughts, I glanced instinctively skyward, past the line of blackened ponderosa pines. Right at the skyline where that orange and black funnel had first appeared above Rose Valley on that terrible day.

My stomach clenched. My muscles also, twitching out of control. I was sickened with dread.

It was so easy to lapse into a fear state. To imagine the giant billowing plume materializing, sudden and unbelievable. It was only a month and a half ago. Just looking at the ridge gripped me with terror.

A month? Seriously? It had to be longer than that. Picturing the roiling cloud, I shivered, although it was still summer warm in Kelowna, even in the early-fall afternoon.

It didn't seem safe out here anymore. I turned and went back inside the house.

32

FINDING THE PHOENIX

A year later, we were finally getting the last of the home repairs done. Everything inside was finished at last, and so we were working on the outside. Landscapers were coming this morning with new plants to replace the incinerated foliage (I particularly mourned the huge, lush, hydrangea bushes, with their ivory blooms).

James, our assigned landscape gardener, was competent and courteous. I was very excited about getting plants and making the front yard beautiful again. James had helped me with the garden design, selecting varieties that were more deer resistant. Although we'd noticed the deer were less picky since the wildfire. Beggars can't be choosers.

All our lighting wires were toast (literally), so we were getting new landscape lights as well. Now that most of the work was done, I was feeling more optimistic about life. It also helped that so many of the new builds were springing up all around us.

A doe and her fawns navigate their way through construction equipment on our burned-out street

Survivor's guilt doesn't evaporate overnight. But if you greet some of your neighbours—like we recently did—and they have big smiles on their faces as they contemplate their brand-new home nearing completion (with the assessment value rising substantially) the guilt has a way of becoming manageable.

Plus, I'd committed to writing a memoir. I was still feeling scattered. And there was so much to do, including publishing another completed book. But this was an important part of our neighbourhood's healing.

Here goes, I thought, opening a "New Book" folder on my computer.

As I BEGAN TYPING the first draft of this memoir, there were many things I didn't yet know, past and future. For instance, months after we returned home, I stumbled across the following article, written right before the McDougall Creek fire morphed into the largest wildfire West Kelowna has ever seen—breaking the record set by the fire they talk about in this piece, which occurred twenty years before, *to the very day.*

Excerpt from BCTV News, August 15, 2023

...On August 16, 2003, a lightning strike sparked a fire near Okanagan Mountain Provincial Park, that grew to spurring evacuations of more than 33,000 residents and damaging or destroying more than 200 homes.

At the time, the 2003 season was unprecedented in scale, but it has been dwarfed this year by fires that burned six times more area...

I'd heard about the fire, from residents and firefighters. But It's a pretty eerie co-incidence that they both started the same day, twenty years apart. It's enough to make you shake your head in disbelief.

Stranger still, *even as that reporter typed those words*, the McDougall Creek fire was gearing up for its destructive rampage across the hillsides of West Kelowna.

*Side note: The Okanagan Mountain wildfire that took place two decades ago (2003) was sparked by lightning. But the jury is still out on what started the McDougall Creek wildfire.

Was it human caused? We may never know.

AS FOR THE FUTURE? Some things have been surprising, some not.

Not at all surprising is the fact that West Kelowna Fire Chief Jason Brolund won multiple awards and acclaim for his role in protecting our community from the McDougall Creek wildfire: the highly prestigious Governor General Award and the King Charles Award, among others.

In late September, 2023, Fire Chief Brolund was asked to speak at the United Nations during the Climate Change summit in New York, where he told delegates that climate change has become very real for Kelowna residents.

West Kelowna Fire Chief Jason Brolund speaking at the U.N.

To quote from his speech:

I want to take you back with me to a hot, windy August night. We were surrounded by fire. Wind was driving it down on us. The sky was orange. We were dug in, it was the fight of our lives.

"We ordered over 10,000 people to get out that night…Some people made it to the lake, their only option to survive in the water…Not all doors were knocked on, the fire came too fast," he said, adding that he has never stopped thinking about the difficult decision to put firefighters in harm's way.

He also recalled how firefighters saved an entire row of homes with a crew of only eight and how, despite all odds, a $75-million new water treatment plant.

"Climate change became very real for West Kelowna on August 16," he said. "Over $20 million was spent reacting to my fire, not to mention the insurance losses which could be triple that."

He questioned what could have been accomplished if that money had been spent proactively fighting the climate change.

"We're spending money on the wrong end of the problem."

Food for thought.

ALSO NOT SURPRISING for Royal Heights Properties residents, frustration and disappointment in large doses lay ahead, for both 'total loss' owners and the 'still standing' people. Dealing with home insurance companies was like being slowly flayed alive. But enough about that. Lots of positive stuff happened after we got home—and continues to happen.

Like Mo and Mike's baby, who came into the world a few months ago, healthy and beautiful. Plus, their new house is close to completion. It looks fantastic and is almost move-in ready.

Aleda and Joseph also are rebuilding, but it took a while to decide, and who can blame them? I still shudder when I think about their burned car skeletons.

Steve and Tracy moved into their new home a couple of weeks ago. We brought them flowers and wine; Tracy and I had a tear-filled hug.

Chantelle and Tim's place has been among the last in our community to get going because of frustrating delays—which took a major toll on them. But now it's being built at last, and they'll be home by this summer. We'll get to wave at Nash as he jumps on his trampoline, and play with Jax when he comes sneaking through the hole in the fence.

Oliver won't be here for that. Unexpected and sad, we lost our beloved pooch last year. He was the best evacuation therapy dog, ever.

On a happier note, our bonds with our neighbours in Royal Heights Properties have continued to strengthen because of our shared calamity. It's no exaggeration to say that we have forged some deep friendships that will last a lifetime.

More and more wildlife are returning to the area. The resilience of these animals is astounding and inspiring. Every time I see a doe nudge her fawn down the slippery slope of the burned gully, searching for the tasty fresh shoots that have sprung up, I am awestruck. It harkens me back to the reverential way Chief Louie spoke of the animals who share this earth with us.

Hundreds of burned trees have recently been removed from the surrounding hillside in Royal Heights. It's distressing to see the massive gaps where there used to be dense forest. But it's necessary. Besides being hazardous, burned trees aren't fun to look at.

Rebirth and regrowth are in the air. Finding the Phoenix isn't so elusive now. It's everywhere, as long as you're willing to see it.

Or hear it.

This morning I thought I heard a familiar sound, so I went outside.

And there was Stella, sitting on the fence, bright blue feathers stirring, head cocked as she gazed at me, waiting for her peanut. A year after the McDougall Creek wildfire evacuation, almost to the day.

It was like she'd never been gone.

THE END

AFTERWORD

I hope you found this story interesting, even if you were not directly affected by the McDougall Creek wildfire.

If you did, please consider leaving a review. Reader feedback is gold for authors, and I would greatly appreciate it if you could take the time to say a few words about your reading experience —even a couple of lines, at any of the following links:

http://www.amazon.com/review/create-review?&asin=173827781X

https://www.judithlepore.com

https://linktr.ee/judithlepore

ACKNOWLEDGMENTS

Thank you to Fire Chief Jason Brolund, Mayor Gord Milsom, and Westbank First Nation Chief Robert Louie, all of whom worked tirelessly for weeks to protect our community from the scourge of the McDougall Creek wildfire.

Thank you to the friends who took us in, those who offered to take us in, and those who were just there in the background, rooting for us to be okay.

And as always, thanks to our families, for whom we live and breathe, making it always worthwhile to keep going...

I also gratefully acknowledge the folks at Castanet newspaper, on whose data I relied on heavily, both as a terrified evacuee scrambling for scraps of news, and then later as an emotionally-laden chronicler of this wildfire ordeal, who still wanted to get her facts straight. The Castanet staff were courteous and helpful as I strove to find the right pictures and quotes to accurately depict my evacuation odyssey (Colin Dacre in particular).

This gratitude extends also to all the other local, provincial, and national news sources I cited.

While putting the finishing touches on this memoir, I had the privelege of meeting with Fire Chief Jason Brolund and Mayor Gord Milsom, as well as Chief Robert Louie of the Westbank First Nation, on whose land we reside.

They were kind and encouraging, graciously taking the time to read my book draft, offer insights, and express their belief that this very personal account of the McDougall Creek wildfire should be told.

When I asked them about what residents in high-risk communities could do to reduce the threat of wildfire destruction to their properties, Fire Chief Brolund was very clear: Everyone should be familiar with the Fire Smart Principles, and abide by them.

It can be as simple as taking a one hour free online Fire Smart course:

https://firesmartbc.ca/events/category/course/

You can also get an assessment of your home from the Wildfire Mitigation Program:

https://firesmartbc.ca/wmp/

Chief Robert Louie, Mayor Milsom, and Fire Chief Brolund, also hope for an increase in government budgeting for the *prevention of wildfires*, rather than the focus being on reparations after the disaster has occurred.

A percentage of the proceeds from this book will be donated toward that efffort.

ABOUT THE AUTHOR

Judith Lepore hails from Vancouver, Canada, and is the published author of an epic fantasy trilogy "The Magic of Miraven," which garnered stellar reviews, and has enjoyed sales in eight countries.

Prior to publishing her novels, Judith worked for three decades as a freelance writer and editor in film, radio, and television. Passionate about health and fitness, she also wrote a monthly fitness column for several years in her local newspaper.

Accomplishing all this while raising two children and working as a personal trainer, Judith has led a busy life. Finally, in 2022, she and her husband Lorenzo pursued a long-held dream and moved to West Kelowna, B.C.

The following summer, the horrendous McDougall Creek wildfire descended on the region. It remains the Okanagan's worst wildfire on record.

Because Judith's neighborhood was among the hardest hit, she felt compelled to chronicle her story of a month-long evacuation, and her community's struggle to overcome the ensuing devastation and trauma.

To see Judith's other books, or drop her a line, you can reach her at this author website:

https://www.judithlepore.com

www.ingramcontent.com/pod-product-compliance
Lightning Source LLC
Chambersburg PA
CBHW071958070526
44583CB00015B/1240